The New King James Version: In the Great Tradition

Arthur L. Farstad

Thomas Nelson Publishers
Nashville

Printed in the United States of America

ISBN 0-8407-3148-5

2 3 4 5 6 7 8 9 10 - 97 96 95 94 93 92 91

Acknowledgments

I wish to express my deep thanks to my colleague Dr. William McDowell, English Editor of the New King James Version, for his most helpful suggestions and editorial expertise in the preparation of this book.

My deep gratitude also goes to my fellow language-editor, Dr. James D. Price, Executive Old Testament Editor of the New King James, for his research and help in the historical and Hebraic parts of this book.

And I thank my nephew, Mark J. Farstad, for his splendid job of turning my cryptic handwriting into clean computer copy.

CONTENTS

PART ONE: Accuracy

PART TWO: Beauty

PART THREE: Completeness

FOREWORD

A *New* King James? What's new? What changes were made and why? Who was involved in the project? Did they believe in the inspiration, inerrancy, and infallibility of the Scriptures? Were the original languages considered? How long did it take to do all of this? Who paid for it? Why a New King James? Why not a completely new translation?

All of these questions and many more are answered in *The New King James Version: In the Great Tradition.* It would be hard to imagine a more qualified author for this work than Dr. Arthur Farstad, whose education and experience eminently qualify him for the task. He earned a Th.M. in Old Testament and Th.D. in New Testament from Dallas Theological Seminary. A teacher of Greek, Dr. Farstad was appointed New Testament Editor for the New King James Version and was later named Executive Editor for the whole project. As such, he played an integral role in the development of both the Old and the New Testament. Moreover, I personally know Dr. Farstad to be not only a scholar but also a deeply spiritual man.

You will enjoy reading this book. In a most delightful manner, it will answer all your questions concerning the New King James Version. You may be surprised to discover that the "authorized" 1611 edition of the King James Version was never formally authorized by any group, either sacred or secular; that William Shakespeare was consulted on the poetry of the Psalms; and that for 80 years after its publication in 1611 the King James Version was bitterly attacked. You can even find out what version of the Bible was used at the wedding of Prince Charles and Lady Diana! Dr. Farstad covers the New King James from *A* to *Z.*

Every user of the New King James Version ought to read this volume, as should those flirting with using it. "Non-NKJVers" will profit, too, from the wealth of information about Bible history and translation.

Years ago, in his book, *Where Did We Get Our Bible?*, Dr. George L. Robinson called the original King James Version of 1611 "a monumental, literary masterpiece, which, for rhythm and cadence, will ever hold a very high place in the catalogue of Bible revisions." This book explains how the New King James Version continues that great tradition.

Dr. Michael Cocoris
Senior Pastor
Church of the Open Door
Glendora, Claifornia

Introduction

"Oh, no sir, you wouldn't want *The New King James*—they merely went through the old King James and changed the *thees* and *thous* to *yous* and *thems*!" (sic).

The scene was a denominational bookstore in a large and famous U.S. city. The speaker was a saleslady and the would-be NKJV-buyer was a young Bible marketing man who already knew far more than she about the version in question.

Now if the NKJV had been a government project, using public tax money, we could easily believe that over 130 people from all over the English-speaking world might spend seven years and over $4 million and do only as much as the lady suggested. Actually, this was the amount of privately funded time and labor spent in producing the NKJV, which was the fifth *major* revision of the original Authorized Version in over three hundred years.[1] It is an interesting note that the initial translation of 1611 also took seven years to produce.

All of the translators, editors, and reviewers of the NKJV text were competent Christian scholars dedicated to the highest view of biblical inspiration. Also believing in the need for continuity, they were deeply committed to preserving the revered King James tradition for present and future generations of Bible readers. As for the cost, all was provided by Thomas Nelson Publishers, Nashville, Tennessee. Initial funds were made possible by previous sales of a patriotic volume[2] celebrating the 200th birthday of the U.S.A.

After struggling with the archaic and obsolete vocabulary and phrasing in the King James Version, young Joe Moore asked his father, President of Thomas Nelson, "Daddy, you make so many Bibles, why can't you make a Bible that I can understand?" This question was the genesis of the NKJV.

Founded in 1798 in Edinburgh, Thomas Nelson had already pioneered the English Revised Version (1885), the American Standard Version (1901), and the Revised Standard Version (1952). After Mr. Sam Moore bought the company in 1969, he wanted to contribute a Bible that was understandable to young people like Joe and yet retained the great tradition of the Tyndale-King James Bible in text and style.

No easy task!

Across North America and in a few talks abroad it has been my privilege to present the virtues of the NKJV on radio and TV, to pastors, prison workers, Bible people, publishers, churches, para-church societies, colleges, and seminaries. Since so many had a part in this Bible, I trust no one will find it in poor taste for the Executive Editor to draw attention to its qualities. The NKJV is well worth your consideration as your everyday, standard Bible.

Over the years I have sought to reduce my presentation to two main considerations: *Readability* and *Reliability.* We will briefly cover the first in this Introduction.

Readability

A great work of literature could conceivably be accurate in its presentation, beautiful in style, complete in text—and yet be *unreadable!* If my former English literature teachers will forgive my mentioning it, I seem to remember a few very long seventeenth-century poems that fit that very description!

The name "New King James Version" can be stressed on the *New* part or the *King James* part. Both are true. If the latter is stressed too much, people get the impression that the NKJV is difficult for most readers (as are earlier editions of the KJV in many places). If we overstress the *New* aspect, people could get the idea that we have an entirely new version. This is not true. A sufficiently large part of the King James tradition is retained to merit our name. Yet there are enough changes in the work to make it much more readable. But what is "readability"?

Readability is the degree of ease with which printed matter can be read. Tests that measure the reading level of printed matter usually express their results in terms of the public school's system of grade levels. Thus, material that has a sixth-grade reading level can comfortably be read by a normal sixth-grade pupil.

Different readability tests measure different characteristics of reading material. For example, the Dale-Chall Formula counts the number of words in a test passage which do *not* appear on the Dale list of three thousand words, then combines that information with the number of words and sentences in the passage. The Fry Formula is based on the number of syllables, words, and sentences in the sample. The Raygor Formula is based on the number of words with six or more letters and the number of words and sentences.

We must be careful in measuring the reading level of an English Bible translation because biblical literature is so diverse in kinds of prose and poetry. For its study of reading level, the editors of the New King James Version obtained the services of a specialist in language arts and reading, Dr. Nancy McAleer.[3]

Consideration was given to the different kinds of literature found in the Bible. Two sample passages each were selected from narrative passages, instructive passages, and poetic passages, a total of six test selections. Both Old and New Testament passages were used.

To these six passages were applied three different reading tests: the Dale-Chall Formula, the Fry Formula, and the Raygor Formula. Actual scores on the individual passages ranged from low-fifth grade to mid-tenth grade.

Individual scores were then averaged, and the results were presented in bar graphs. These bar graphs, included here, report in two ways the reading level of the New King James Version. Figure 1 shows the reading level of the New King James Version as measured by each test. Figure 2 illustrates the average reading level of different types of literature in the New King James Version. Figure 3 is a comparison of the reading level of several English versions of the Bible.

As seen by Figures 1 and 2, the reading level of the New King James Version is high-seventh to low-eighth grade.

By comparison, the reading level of samples from a daily newspaper in a U.S. metropolitan area showed a range from eleventh grade to college. Instructions for preparing a TV dinner were written at the eighth-grade level. Directions for taking aspirin were written at the tenth-grade level. The rules for completing a "simplified" income tax form measured above the twelfth-grade level.

Reliability

Conceivably a Bible might be accurate, beautiful, and complete—yet be very hard to read. On the other hand it could be very readable, yet be lacking in accuracy, beauty, or completeness (perhaps all three!). There are such Bibles. A few are published to promote some diluted versions of the Christian faith. The style of some is pretty, but they are also loose and inaccurate. One or two might be correct and yet weak in English style.

The rest of this little volume is intended to show that we didn't just "change the *thee*s and *thou*s"! The translators, editors, Executive Review Committees, and Overview Committees worked conscientiously together as teams of qualified Christian scholars. They were striving to produce a faithful update of the Tyndale-King James tradition that could truly be considered to possess the ABC's of good Bible translation:

Accuracy
Beauty
Completeness

These were our goals.

charts

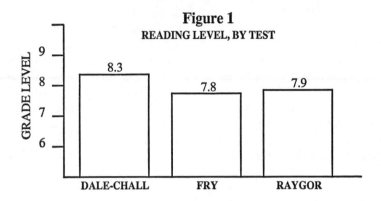

Figure 1
READING LEVEL, BY TEST

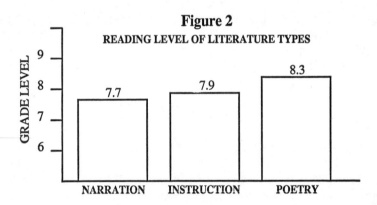

Figure 2
READING LEVEL OF LITERATURE TYPES

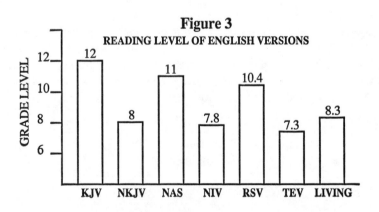

Figure 3
READING LEVEL OF ENGLISH VERSIONS

NOTES

[1]The *Revised Standard Version* and the *New American Standard Version* are revisions, not of the King James, but of the *American Standard Version.* The ASV was the U.S. variation of the *English Revised Version.* The ERV was supposed to be a revision of the Authorized Version with only absolutely necessary changes to insure accuracy. (The Old English was retained.) However, the New Testament was translated from the Greek text of Westcott and Hort, not the Textus Receptus of the KJV. Since this departure was not a part of the translators' assignment, it was criticized—probably rightly so.

[2]*The Bicentennial Almanac,* edited by Calvin D. Linton.

[3]Dr. McAleer is the chairwoman of the Department of Education and Human Development, and associate professor at Rollins College, Winter Park, Florida.

PART ONE:

ACCURACY

"He spoke and taught accurately the things of the Lord" (Acts 18:25).

Surveys among Bible buyers and readers indicate that the leading concern of those who love God's Word is that a version of the Scriptures be a translation that is *accurate.* If a Bible isn't presenting exactly what God communicated to His people through the forty or so writers whom He graciously inspired to write His Word, to that degree it is a failure.

Clearly, on the one hand, it is difficult to enjoy a rendering of the Bible that rigidly ignores English idiom and good style—resembling the translation on a page of an interlinear Testament. On the other hand, we readily reject any professed translation of God's Word that takes such liberties that it is more truly a paraphrase or commentary than a translation. As the late Dr. Harry Sturz, textual scholar and beloved member of the NKJV New Testament Executive Review Committee, used to say, "We want a Bible that gives us what the text *says,* not what some scholar thinks it *means!*"

The NKJV, following firmly in the footsteps of the Authorized or King James Version, is just such a desired Bible. The following chapters will make this evident:

1. A Firm Foundation. In this first chapter we present the excellent contributions of the English translations from the fourteenth to the early seventeenth centuries that culminated in one of the most highly esteemed Bibles in any language, the Authorized Version.

2. A Royal Legacy: The King James Version. Chapter 2 gives a brief survey of how this great Bible came to be, how it is actually a revision of previous works, and has itself been revised a number of times.

3. Rewiring the House. Building on a metaphor from J. B. Phillips, Chapter 3 examines how and why the New King James was designed to keep the tradition current as we face the twenty-first century.

4. Finishing Touches. Chapter 4 gives examples of important details that make the NKJV an outstandingly accurate Bible version.

1

A Firm Foundation

The New King James Version, as the name implies, is not a completely new translation, but a conservative and careful revision of that most influential Bible translation in any modern language, the Authorized or King James Version. What is not nearly so well known is that the King James Bible itself was not a new version, even when it appeared in 1611. That translation, too, was a conservative and careful revision of several English Bibles produced and revised between 1526 and 1610. Many Christians know little of how much blood,[1] sweat, and tears went into the great English Bible tradition that we enjoy. The story is worth telling.

Even though the first complete English Bible had very little effect on the Tyndale—King James/New King James continuum, for completeness we would like to start with that "morning star of the Reformation," John Wycliffe.

The First Wycliffe Translator (1382)

The Wycliffe Bible Translators are known around the world for their much-needed and splendid work of putting God's Word into the minority languages and dialects of the world—not only in the Third World, but also in the native tongues of North, Central, and South America. The organization is named after the scholarly Oxford don who can truly be called the first "Wycliffe" translator—John Wycliffe himself (1320?-1384). Wycliffe translated his New Testament very literally from the Latin Vulgate, not from the original Greek. Thus it was a translation of a translation, and naturally lost some precision in the process. Nevertheless, it was a landmark in Bible translation nearly a century before the invention of printing. The entire Bible was later finished with the help of other scholars, such as William Hereford. Many copies were made by hand, but it was dangerous to possess even a page of this manuscript because of ecclesiastical opposition to God's Word in the language of the people.

The King James tradition retains only a few Wycliffe renderings, since the seventeenth-century translators were not revising his translation, but rather the Tyndale and later Bibles until 1610. Three interesting Wycliffe renderings are: "the sword of the ghost," "a good knight of Jesus Christ," and "the helm of helth" (the helmet of salvation).

Treasures from Tyndale

Cuthbert Tonstall, bishop of London, was hosting a bonfire in front of St. Paul's Cathedral in London. What was that cleric burning? Bibles! Indeed, they were the first printed New Testaments in English (1526), translated by William Tyndale. We suspect that the bishop would have liked to have cast Tyndale into the flames too. But that came later. The prelate had two goals: to buy up and burn Tyndale's New Testament, and to squelch the movement towards biblical reform.

Tonstall succeeded fairly well in his first goal—only two or three copies of Tyndale's first edition exist today.[2] Ironically, the money that the bishop spent on the first edition helped to finance an improved edition. (Later editions are a part of *all* major English Bibles, even if sometimes used only for the purpose of correcting details.) And of course the bishop's second objective was a failure. Biblical reform did go forward, in answer to godly Tyndale's dying prayer.

Since Tyndale is such an important figure in the KJV/NKJV story, we would like to give the highlights of his remarkable ministry.

Tyndale's Translating Ministry

William Tyndale (1494?–1536) was from a well-to-do family and received his B.A. degree from Oxford in 1512. His M.S. degree was conferred in 1515. Tyndale then left Oxford for Cambridge where he spent about seven years. At Cambridge he was inspired to study Greek and theology. He was also influenced by John Colet's literal method of interpreting Scripture in opposition to the allegorical method used by the church. It was evidently the influence of Erasmus of Rotterdam that impressed Tyndale with a great urgency to translate God's Word into the language of his own people. Erasmus had published a Greek New Testament in 1516 that became a basis of Luther's Bible on the Continent. Tyndale's desire was no doubt enhanced by the appearance of Luther's German translation in 1522.

Once, while debating, a certain learned man told him, "We were better to be without God's laws than the pope's." Tyndale answered, "I defy the pope and all his laws; if God spare my life, ere many years, I will cause a boy that driveth the plow shall know more of the Scripture than thou doest."[3]

Tyndale determined to translate from the original Greek and Hebrew, and for this task he was eminently qualified. He was fluent, not only in Hebrew, Greek, and Latin, but also in Italian, Spanish, English, French, and German.

As we have seen, the bishop of London opposed Tyndale's idea of an authorized English Bible, and it soon became apparent that there was no possibility of making his translation in England. So, in 1524, Tyndale sailed for Germany where he translated his New Testament in the safety of Lutheran Wittenburg. He would never again see the shores of his native England.

Unlike modern scholars Tyndale had very few technical helps, such as grammars, lexicons, and other scholarly works. He had no Greek manuscripts, and his only Greek New Testament was the third edition of Erasmus' work. Tyndale's rendering was independent and refreshingly original, based neither on Wycliffe nor on any other work. It was a Bible intended for the people, not for scholars.

When his work on the New Testament was nearing completion, Tyndale moved to Cologne to print the first edition. His enemies halted the printing, but he was able to escape to Worms with a supply of the first ten sheets (eighty pages) which he published separately in 1525. These pages contain Tyndale's Prologue and most of Matthew's Gospel. The only surviving copy is in the British Museum.

In the spring of 1526, the first edition of Tyndale's New Testament (6,000 copies) came off the press—*the first complete English New Testament ever printed.* Most of these were smuggled into England. But in October 1526, as we have seen, the bishop of London ordered all copies of Tyndale's New Testament destroyed.

Old Testament Work (1530)

During the next four years Tyndale evidently learned Hebrew from Jewish rabbis in Germany and began translating the Old Testament. At Marburg, on January 17, 1530, he published his first Old Testament work, the Pentateuch. As with the New Testament, Tyndale had few scholarly resource materials for translating from Hebrew. His Hebrew text was probably the recently printed second Bomberg edition of the Rabbinic Bible (1525).

Soon after publishing the Pentateuch, Tyndale moved to the safe sanctuary afforded foreign merchants within the walls of the free city of Antwerp. In 1531 he published the Book of Jonah, and in 1534 he produced a second edition of the Pentateuch. He continued to translate the Old Testament, but no more of it was published during his lifetime.

Tyndale's Revised New Testament (1535, 1536)

In addition to his work on the Old Testament, Tyndale worked extensively on improving the New Testament. In November of 1534 he published his first revised edition and in 1535 the second revised edition of the New Testament. This was his final work of publication.

Tyndale's Martyrdom (1536)

In late May of 1535, Tyndale was lured outside the safety of the walls of the free city by a false friend and betrayed to officers. He was then taken prisoner to the Castle of Vilford, where he remained until his death, there continuing his translation of the Old Testament to the end of 1 and 2 Chronicles. Although he was unable to finish the Old Testament, Tyndale evidently translated portions of other Old Testament books.

In August of 1536, Tyndale was sentenced to die the death of a heretic—strangulation and burning at the stake. The infamous sentence was carried out on October 6, 1536, after the saintly martyr cried out his last prayer, "Lord, open the King of England's eyes!"

Tyndale's dying prayer was soon answered. Before the end of 1537 the first volume of the English Bible ever printed in England (Tyndale's translation with a few changes) came off the presses of the king's own printer, and was made available to the common people of England. Now it was indeed possible for a plowboy to read and know God's Word in his native tongue!

Tyndale's Biblical Legacy

The debt that lovers of the Bible owe to Tyndale can scarcely be overstated. R. Demaus, a biographer of the translator, writes:

> The English New Testament, as we now have it, is, in its substance, the unchanged language of Tyndale's first version. The English Bible has been subjected to repeated revisions; the scholarship of generations, better provided than Tyndale was with critical apparatus, has been brought to bear upon it; writers, by no means overly-friendly to the original translator, have had it in their power to disparage and displace his work; yet, in spite of all these influences, that Book to which all Englishmen turn as the source, and the guide, and the stay of their spiritual life, is still substantially the translation of Tyndale. And most emphatically may it be said of those passages of the New Testament which are most intimately associated with our deepest

religious emotions, that it is the actual unchanged words of the original translator which are treasured up in our hearts, and are so potent in impressing the soul.[4]

Comparing Tyndale's Work

Since Tyndale's work is so very foundational to our traditions, we feel it is worth giving a selection of his New Testament (John 14:1-11) compared with the 1611 KJV and the NKJV. Fully ninety percent of the King James New Testament is Tyndale's wording. For the sake of historical interest we retain the sixteenth-century spelling in Tyndale's column and the seventeenth-century spelling in the King James column. For convenience we have added the verse numbers to Tyndale's text.

Tyndale (1526)	KJV (1611)	NKJV (1985)
1 AND he sayde vnto hys disciples: Lett nott youre hertes be trubled. Beleve in God and beleve in me.	1 Let not your heart be troubled: yee beleeue in God, beleeue also in me.	1 "Let not your heart be troubled; you believe in God, believe also in Me.
2 In my fathers housse are many mansions. If it were not soo/ I wolde have tolde you. I goo to prepare a place for you.	2 In my Fathers house are many mansions; if it were not so, I would haue told you: I goe to prepare a place for you.	2 "In My Father's house are many mansions; if it were not so, I would have told you. I go to prepare a place for you.
3 I will come agayne/ and receve you even vnto my selfe/that where I am/ theare maye ye be also.[5]	3 And if I goe and prepare a place for you, I will come againe, and receiue you vnto my selfe, that where I am, there ye may be also.	3 "And if I go and prepare a place for you, I will come again and receive you to Myself; that where I am, there you may be also.
4 And whither I goo ye knowe/and the waye ye knowe.	4 And whither I goe yee know, and the way ye know.	4 "And where I go you know, and the way you know."
5 Thomas sayde vnto him: Lorde we knowe not whyther thou goest. Also how is it possible for vs to knowe the waye?	5 Thomas saith vnto him, Lord, we know not whither thou goest: and how can we know the way?	5 Thomas said to Him, "Lord, we do not know where You are going, and how can we know the way?"
6 Iesus sayd vnto him: I am the waye/ verite/ and lyfe. Noman cometh vnto the father/but by me.	6 Iesus saith vnto him, I am the Way, the Trueth, and the Life: no man commeth vnto the Father but by mee.	6 Jesus said to him, "I am the way, the truth, and the life. No one comes to the Father except through Me

7 Yf ye had knowen me ye had knowen my father alsoo. And nowe ye knowe him. And ye have sene him.

8 Phillip said vnto him: lorde shew vs thy father/ and it suffiseth vs.

9 Iesus sayde vnto him: have I bene so longe time with you: and yet hast thou not knowen me? Philip/ he that hath sene me/ hath sene the father. And howe sayest thou then: shewe vs the father?

10 Belevest thou nott that I am in the father/ and the father in me? The wordes that I speake vnto you/ I speake not of my silfe: but the father dwellinge in me is he that doeth the workes.

11 Beleve me that I am in the father and the father in me. Att the leest beleve me for the very workes sake.

7 If ye had knowen me, ye should haue knowen my Father also: and from henceforth ye know him, and haue seene him.

8 Philip sayth vnto him, Lord, shew vs the Father, and it sufficeth vs.

9 Iesus saith vnto him, Haue I bin so long time with you, and yet hast thou not knowen me, Philip? he that hath seene me, hath seene the father, and how sayest thou then, Shew vs the father?

10 Beleeuest thou not that I am in the father, and the father in mee? The words that I speake vnto you, I speake not of my selfe: but the Father that dwelleth in me, he doth the works.

11 Beleeue me that I am in the Father, and the Father in mee: or else beleeue me for the very workes sake.

7 If you had known Me, you would have known My Father also; and from now on you know Him and have seen Him."

8 Philip said to Him, "Lord, show us the Father, and it is sufficient for us."

9 Jesus said to him, "Have I been with you so long, and yet you have not known Me, Philip? He who has seen Me has seen the Father, so how can you say, 'Show us the Father'?

10 "Do you not believe that I am in the Father, and the Father in Me? The words that I speak to you I do not speak on My own authority; but the Father who dwells in Me does the works.

11 "Believe Me that I am in the Father and the Father in Me, or else believe Me for the sake of the works themselves.

Tyndale's Contribution to English

What Luther's Bible did for German, what Calvin's *Institutes* and *Commentaries* did for French to a lesser degree, Tyndale's Bible did for the English tongue. Demaus explains:

Even as a literary work the issue of Tyndale's translation forms an important era in our history. At a time when the English language was still unformed; when it had not as yet been the vehicle of any great literary undertaking; when men of learning still looked upon it as an imperfect instrument, fit only for commonplace purposes, Tyndale showed that its capacity was unbounded; that in simplicity, majesty, strength, musical flow, ability to relate gracefully and perspicuously, to touch the feelings, to awe by its solemnity, to express the highest truths in the clearest words, it yields to no other language ancient or modern. . . in thus holding up before the nation, in a book which has become sanctified by the reverence of ten generations, a model of the highest literary excellence, simple, honest, and manly; free alike from the pedantry of the verbal scholar, and the affected point and force of the mere man of letters, he has exercised a permanent influence of the most beneficial kind over the literary taste of the English people.[6]

From Tyndale to King James

Some people incorrectly say that the Authorized Version assumed supremacy because it had no rivals. Indeed, several complete Protestant Bibles and one Roman Catholic Bible appeared between 1534 and 1610. Most of these used Tyndale's base to a greater or lesser degree. Besides the Coverdale Bible (1534), there was the Matthew Bible (1537), the Taverner Bible (1539), the Great Bible (1539), the Geneva Bible (1560), the Bishops' Bible (1568), and the Roman Catholic Douai-Rheims Bible (1609–10). Each Bible had some good features and phrases that are still current in the KJV/NKJV tradition.

These revisions were due partly to the expedience of making the work acceptable to king and clergy. Until modern times all English Bibles after Tyndale, including the KJV, were revisions of previous editions. An important feature of each revision was a restyling of the language, conforming to current literary usage.

The Coverdale Bible (1534)

Miles Coverdale (1488?–1569) has the distinction of producing the first complete *printed* Bible in the English language. He was ordained a priest about 1526 and became an Augustinian friar. Educated at Cambridge, he came under the influence of the Protestant Reformation but was endangered in the church by his new ideas. So he left the Augustinian order and fled for safety to the Continent, where he lived from 1528 to 1535.

He spent some time in Hamburg helping Tyndale with his work, and again later in Antwerp as a proofreader. Led to produce his own English Bible, Coverdale modified Tyndale's New Testament and Pentateuch with only minor revisions. But Tyndale's translation of Joshua through Chronicles was not available, so he translated the rest of the Old Testament and the Apocrypha from the Latin, also using available German versions.

Because the Coverdale Bible appeared on the scene at an opportune time,

15

it was not opposed. Nobody noticed that it contained the "heretic" Tyndale's work, and it was an immediate success with the people. The second edition (1537), under license of the king, seems a direct answer to Tyndale's dying prayer.

Although Coverdale's Bible was not translated entirely from the original languages, he did make some significant contributions. Besides editing the first complete English Bible, Coverdale restored such old ecclesiastical words as *church*[7] and *bishop*. He was the first to separate the Apocrypha from the Old Testament, contrary to their arrangement in the Latin Vulgate.[8]

Coverdale's English, especially in the Psalms, is musical and beautifully phrased. His Psalter appeared in the *Book of Common Prayer* for centuries after the KJV had been adopted by the Church of England.

Matthew's Bible (1537)

Tyndale had given John Rogers his unfinished manuscripts of the Old Testament. With these manuscripts plus Coverdale's first edition, Rogers produced his Bible under the fictitious name of Thomas Matthew in order to confuse the Roman Catholic Inquisition. He revised Tyndale's translation of Genesis through Chronicles, plus Jonah, and Tyndale's 1535 New Testament. For the rest of the Old Testament and the Apocrypha he revised Coverdale's translation.

Because Protestant Archbishop Cranmer liked Matthew's Bible, he requested that it be licensed by the king. As a result Matthew's Bible, with a foreword by Cranmer, was published in England in 1537 *under license of the king*—a second answer to Tyndale's prayer.

Returning to England for the publication of his Bible, Rogers experienced success until persecution once again sprang up under "Bloody" Mary Tudor. In 1555 he became the first martyr to be burned at Smithfield during her reign.

The Taverner Bible (1539)

One of the lesser-known Bibles from this era is the work of Richard Taverner. His Bible was a revision of Matthew's Bible. Although it had little effect on later English Bibles, it is worth mentioning for the sake of completeness. Taverner, a layman, was a very competent Greek scholar. His contribution in translating the Greek New Testament was bringing greater accuracy to the English text. This was especially true regarding the definite article, an important item in Greek grammar. One phrase that the King James and New King James owe to this scholarly layman is in Hebrews 1:3 where the Son is called "the express image" of God's person.

The Great Bible (1539)

In 1536 Cranmer again petitioned King Henry VIII to authorize the production of an English Bible suitable for use in the churches. While anticipating such authorization, Thomas Cromwell, then Vicar General to the king, had Coverdale produce a revision of Matthew's Bible with an Old Testament more faithful to the Hebrew, Aramaic, and Greek originals— as well as to several Latin translations. The reformers were disappointed, however, that there was so much Latin influence in this work.

The first edition came out in 1539, in large folio with black letters, without notes. Its name, The Great Bible, was partly due to its large size (11 x 16½ inches) and partly due to its fine workmanship. When the Inquisition tried to halt the work, the finished pages had to be smuggled into England from France, where they were printed.

Thomas Cromwell had prepared the way for the Great Bible in 1538 by issuing an injunction that before a specified day each church should have "one boke of the whole Bible, *in the largest volume,* in Englyshe, sett up in summe convenyent place within the churche that ye have cure of, whereat your parishioners may most commodiously resort to the same and reat yt." This made the Great Bible the only English version authorized to be used in the churches. These Bibles were often chained to the lecterns to prevent their removal.

The Great Bible became very popular, even though its sponsor, Thomas Cromwell, lost favor with the king and was executed in 1540. It went through seven editions in two years and remained dominant for almost thirty years.

The latter years of Henry VIII were characterized by an anti-Protestant reaction. The reformers were not in the royal favor, and the king restricted the use of the English Bible. Except for the Great Bible, English Bibles and Testaments were burned in 1546. Ultimately Rogers, like Cranmer, was martyred. Miles Coverdale narrowly escaped by fleeing England.

The Geneva Bible (1560)

Many Puritans and Calvinists were not fully satisfied with the Great Bible. During the anti-Protestant persecution under "Bloody" Mary, many of these people fled to Geneva, where John Calvin was teaching, and settled there. Some of these exiles undertook to revise thoroughly the Great Bible in order to correct the faults they found in it. The New Testament (1557), a revision of Tyndale's work, was translated by William Whittingham, who was related to Calvin by marriage. The complete Bible was issued in 1560. Whittingham was also a principal contributor to the Old Testament, which was a revision of the 1550 edition of the Great Bible. Others who contributed were John

Knox and Miles Coverdale. The project was supervised by John Calvin and Theodore Beza. All of these revisers were competent Hebrew scholars.

The Bible was printed in clear Roman type, with italics used for words supplied by the translators. Marginal comments with notes, maps, tables, and illustrations were also a prominent feature of this handy-sized Bible. For the first time in any English Bible, verse divisions and numbers were used, following the system introduced by Robert Stephanus. The books of the Apocrypha were separated from the Old Testament, with an introduction clearly stating that they were not canonical.

So successful was the Geneva Bible that it completely overshadowed the Great Bible, which was not printed after 1569. The Geneva translation underwent over 140 editions, the last one in 1644. It retained popularity over the Bishops' Bible and even over the KJV for a generation. Scottish families made this version their household Bible.

The Bishops' Bible (1568)

The superior quality of the Geneva Bible made further use of the Great Bible awkward, if not impossible. Although fully accepted in Scotland and quite popular with the English people, the Geneva Bible was unacceptable to the clergy because of its strong Calvinistic notes. To resolve the problem, Archbishop Matthew Parker proposed that the Great Bible be revised. Parker himself was made editor-in-chief of the revision. He appointed a committee of bishops to do the work with the help of other scholars, thus making the Bishops' Bible the first version to be produced by a *committee*. The bishops were instructed to avoid "bitter notes," and to select refined words in good taste. For example, "wantons and buggerers" (Geneva) became "weaklings and abusers of self with mankind" (1 Corinthians 6:9). A similar guideline was followed by the NKJV translators (see Chapter 8, "Something Blue").

The work was completed in seven years and issued in 1568. Because of the variety of contributors and a lack of coordination, the Bishops' Bible was of uneven merit. Even though it was the least successful of the English versions, it still underwent nineteen editions, the last in 1606. Throughout the translation's forty-year lifespan it was overshadowed by the Geneva Bible and finally replaced by the KJV.

The Douai Bible (1609–10)

If the Anglican bishops were unhappy with the Geneva Bible, the Roman Catholic bishops were appalled. The hierarchy opposed translating the Scriptures into the language of the common people, but the Catholic laity's interest in the Geneva Bible was so great that the bishops decided they had better produce an English Bible for Roman Catholics.

Gregory Martin led a team of scholarly English Jesuits in exile at the Seminary of Douai, France, to do the work. The New Testament was printed at Rheims in 1582, and the complete Bible was printed at Douai in 1609–10. It is generally known as the Douai Version. Although reference was made to Greek, Hebrew, and existing English Bibles, the Douai is really a translation of a translation. It contained many anti-Protestant notes. The Douai Version shows obvious dependence on Tyndale, but its English style is frequently unclear, obscure, and much too "Latin." For example, "The Lord is my Shepherd" (Psalm 23:1, literal Hebrew) comes out "Our Lord ruleth me" (*Dominus regit me,* Latin). Such words as *azymes* and *prepuces* (foreskins) sound odd in a Bible. However, the KJV translators were open-minded enough to use several good Douai readings, and some of the Latin-type words went on to become standard English.

The Douai Bible remained the Bible of English-speaking Roman Catholics until recent times. Its form has been changed by successive revisions, making it much closer to the KJV in phraseology and style.

These varied Bibles, nearly all heavily indebted to the work of Tyndale, laid a firm foundation for the King James or Authorized Version. Each made some contribution in vocabulary, style, phraseology, format, or marginal helps.

In our next chapter we shall consider the construction of the monumental 1611 version itself.

NOTES

[1]This is literally true. Such translators as Tyndale and Rogers were martyred for their efforts.

[2]One is at the Baptist Library in Bristol, England, and one (ironically) at St. Paul's, where the bonfire was held. (Perhaps some Bible-lover rescued a copy from the flames and slipped it into the Cathedral Library!)

[3]W. B. Forbush, ed., *Fox's Book of Martyrs,* p. 178.

[4]R. Demaus, *William Tyndale: A Biography,* revised by Richard Lovett, pp. 133-34.

[5]The first clause is missing in the first edition—probably a printer's error. Notice also, in verse 1, that the translator has added an introductory clause.

[6]Demaus, *Tyndale,* p. 137.

[7]Tyndale used *congregation.*

[8]This practice has been followed in all English Protestant Bibles ever since, if the Apocrypha is included at all.

2

A Royal Legacy

Truly (good Christian Reader) wee neuer thought from the beginning, that we should neede to make a new Translation, nor yet to make of a bad one a good one,...but to make a good one better, or out of many good ones, one principall good one, not iustly to be excepted against; that hath bene our indeauour, that our marke.[1]

Dr. Miles Smith's often-quoted words above underline the important truth that the King James Version was not a new or unique translation in its time, but the culmination of a tradition of nearly a century of English Bible translating. With appropriate modernization we could use his words at the head of the next chapter on the making of the *New* King James as well. Indeed, the words are cited in the Preface to the latter version.

But let's take Smith's words in historical context. He was writing the Preface to the first edition of the Authorized, or as North Americans especially like to call it, the "King James" Version. But who was this King James, and why would anyone want to name a major Bible version after a secular monarch?

To answer these questions we must go back in time nearly four centuries to the early 1600's. England was by then an established Protestant realm, and Bible-reading was not only no longer dangerous but even encouraged by king and clergy.

The Historical Setting

The year was 1603. Within four years the first permanent English settlement in North America would be established—Jamestown, Virginia— named after the same King as the Bible Version. Within seventeen years the first settlement in what is now called New England would be established at Plymouth, Massachusetts. Many of these colonists to the Bay Colony would be fleeing the religious repression of this very same King James. Queen Elizabeth I, the so-called "Virgin Queen," was ending her long and dazzling reign (1558–1603). On her deathbed she requested that her cousin, King James VI of Scotland, should come south to London and become King James I of England. James was unimpressive physically and personally, but he was a scholar.

One of the first and also most significant events of James I's reign was the Conference at Hampton Court held in January of 1604. The Puritans had petitioned the new king for improved conditions in the church. Dr. John Reynolds, President of Corpus Christi College, Oxford, and spokesman for the moderate Puritans, recommended that the king authorize a revision of the Bishops' Bible. The king was receptive to the idea, and a letter was soon written to initiate the work. Though he was himself a learned man in Latin, Greek, and Hebrew, there is no evidence that James had any part in the actual translation itself.

The Translation

Fifty-four prominent Greek and Hebrew scholars of the Church of England[2] were selected and organized into six companies. Two companies were to meet at each of the three great centers of learning (Oxford, Cambridge, and Westminster), each company working on a separate section of the Bible. Forty-nine of the original scholars are known; five are now unknown. All the known ones were fine Greek, Hebrew, Latin, and Aramaic scholars, or at least were proficient in two or three of these languages.

The Dean of Westminster, Dr. Lancelot Andrewes, edited Genesis through Second Samuel. His famous collection of devotions, *Preces Privatae,* is still cherished by many.

Translators' Instructions

The first guideline was to change the Bishops' Bible of 1568 "as little as the truth of the original will admit."

Interestingly enough, detailed studies show that only four percent of the King James Bible is distinctively from that version. About two-thirds of the KJV is actually from Tyndale. This shows the wisdom and good taste of the committees.

The Geneva Bible, and even the Douai-Rheims, also made significant contributions to the final version.

Another important guideline was the rejection of any notes other than those explaining the Hebrew or Greek words. King James, although raised in strongly Presbyterian Scotland, was unhappy with the strongly Calvinistic notes of the Geneva Bible, not to mention the anti-Protestant annotations of the Douai-Rheims.

The Work of Translation

The King James Version continued in the method of translating by committees, a tradition begun by the team that produced the Bishops' Bible. But safeguards were employed to assure quality and uniformity of treatment. Each company completed its work and submitted it to the other five for evaluation. When all questions were resolved the final readings were recorded in a master Bible at each university. This process took about three years.

Each university sent its master Bible to London for a review committee to decide the final form based on the readings in the three master copies. The final review committee consisted of two persons from each university and six bishops appointed by King James. Dr. Miles Smith and Dr. Thomas Bilson, Bishop of Winchester, then made a final review, adding headings and chapter-content notes. This work took almost one year. Finally, as we noted, Dr. Smith wrote the Introduction.

Literary Sources

Like the NKJV of over three centuries later, the KJV was a revision of previous outstanding translations, chiefly of William Tyndale. For the Old Testament, the translators used the rabbinic Hebrew Bibles of 1519 and 1525 and the Hebrew texts found in the Complutensian and Antwerp Polyglots. For the New Testament, printed Greek texts by Erasmus, Stephanus, Beza, and the Complutensian Polyglot were used. They also "diligently compared" and revised all of the available English Bibles, the Septuagint, the Vulgate, the Targum, and versions in other modern languages. In short, these learned men left no stone unturned to produce an accurate, beautiful, and complete Bible.

Part of this beauty, at least in the Psalms, may well be traced to England's most famous poet and dramatist. Though not one of the translators, William Shakespeare was called in as a consultant on the poetry of the Psalms. In appreciation of his contribution, the translators decided to honor the poet in a unique yet cryptic way. If you turn to Psalm 46 in the King James and New King James Versions, then count down forty-six words, you will meet the word "shake." Count up forty-six from the end and you will meet the word "spear." Also, in February of 1611 when the King James Version was first published, Shakespeare (1564–1616) was forty-six years old. (He would turn forty-seven in April of that year.) The four forty-sixes are simply too many to be coincidental, so the story must be true.[3]

Christians and others who admire great literature have praised the Authorized Version with good reason. In the words of Dr. James D. Price, the Old Testament Editor of the NKJV, the work is "unsurpassed in excellence of language, rhythm, cadence, majesty, worshipful reverence, and literary beauty."

The First Edition

This version took seven years to complete. The first edition was issued in February of 1611 in a folio volume with black letter type for the main text. Roman type was used for supplied words (what is now printed in italics). It replaced the Bishops' Bible in the churches and was accepted as the authorized Bible because of the king's involvement in its production. "The 1611 version," writes F. F. Bruce, is "commonly called the Authorized Version, but it was never formally authorized by any competent body either in church or state."[4]

Some devotees of the King James Version today are shocked to find out that, like its predecessors, the 1611 Version included the Apocrypha between the Old and New Testaments. But unlike its predecessors, which clearly stated that the apocryphal books were not part of the canon of Scripture, the 1611 Version contained no comments about the canonicity of the Apocrypha, thus leaving the question open. The Puritans requested that copies be printed *without* the Apocrypha, but to no avail. In 1615 Archbishop Abbott prohibited the issue of Bibles without the Apocrypha. It was not until 1629 that the King James Bible was available both with and without the Apocrypha.

In spite of its impressive origins, the Authorized Version received "mixed reviews" at first. Many of the Puritans, Calvinists, and other strict Protestants were not satisfied with it, and continued to use the Geneva Bible, which remained in print until 1644. It is worth noting that the colonists who founded New England took the Geneva, not the King James Version, with them to the New World. They felt the latter reflected "high church" tendencies. Weigle writes regarding the reception of the new version:

> For eighty years after its publication in 1611, the King James Version endured bitter attacks. It was denounced as theologically unsound and ecclesiastically biased, as truckling to the king and unduly deferring to his belief in witchcraft, as untrue to the Hebrew text and relying too much on the Septuagint.[5]

Ultimately the competition died out, the opposition subsided, and the King James Bible took its place in the hearts of the English-speaking peoples. To this day, over 380 years later, it still remains the most widely-sold[6] English Bible in North America; though each year it declines slightly in popularity because of the constant changes in our spoken and written language.

Later Revisions

Occasionally one sees a sign in front of a church building reading: "We use only the 1611 Authorized King James Version." These churches mean well in seeking to maintain a great tradition. However, regarding "the 1611 version," they are in error. If such readers were to be handed a copy of the real 1611 KJV (or the reprint of the same in Roman type), most of them would be unable to follow the archaic spelling and punctuation. Many would probably be offended to find the Apocrypha included as well.

What they are *really* using is the 1769 revision (or a later Americanized edition of the same from the Bible Society). Quite frankly, we should rejoice that they are! It is enough of a hurdle for young people to grope for God's message "through a glass darkly" of 1611 diction. The obsolete spelling and punctuation of the real 1611 edition are very discouraging obstacles to modern reading.

The NKJV is simply the most recent in a series of conservatively revised editions of the Authorized Version. The previous ones were as follows:

The Cambridge Revision of 1629

The King James Bible had been sharply—even viciously—attacked, especially by a certain Hugh Broughton. While Mr. Broughton was a competent scholar, his irascible personality had kept him off the original translation committee. Translators have enough to do with untangling difficulties in translation without having to put up with hard-to-handle committee members. Careless printing and irresponsible editing had left the text of the translation in a poor state, hence a complete revision of the text was undertaken at Cambridge University. The unknown revisers repaired much of the damage done in previous years. They made many changes and corrections of their own, most of which were very valuable.

The Cambridge Revision of 1638

The text was again carefully revised for the second Cambridge edition of 1638. This revision seems to have completed the intent and purpose of the preliminary work of 1629. One of the revisers was Mr. John Boise, one of the original translators who had served in the second Cambridge company. He had later been transferred to the *first* Cambridge company to help finish their section.

The Planned Revision of 1653–1657

In 1653, scarcely more than forty years after the first issue of the Authorized Version, the Long Parliament entertained a bill for a new revision of the Bible. The bill aroused a great deal of interest, and after some delay a subcommittee was appointed in 1657 to work out the details of the revision. However, when Parliament adjourned, the project was set aside. So this revision came to nothing.

The Cambridge Revision of 1762

The English language underwent many changes in spelling, punctuation, vocabulary, and grammar in the 150 years that followed the first edition of the King James Version. In order to restore the Bible to current literary English, a third revision was undertaken at Cambridge by Dr. Thomas Paris, Fellow of Trinity College. He meticulously corrected the italicized words[7] and modernized and regularized both spelling and punctuation. He added 383 marginal notes, many cross references, and Bishop Lloyd's chronological data.

Unfortunately this edition had very limited circulation because a large portion of the printing was destroyed by fire, and the revision was superseded by the Oxford revision of 1769.

The Oxford Revision of 1769

Seven years after the Cambridge revision Dr. Benjamin Blayney, Regius Professor of Hebrew at Oxford, made a similar one. He worked for about four years, collating the then current editions of Oxford and Cambridge with those of 1611 and 1701. Blayney wanted to restore the text of the English Bible to its original purity. He incorporated most of the revisions of Dr. Paris and made many more of his own. He further revised the punctuation and use of italics. This revision, as we noted, is the edition of the King James that most people possess today.

An American Attempt (1833)

The King James Bible probably has had an even deeper impact on the United States and Canada than in its country of origin. The reason for this is that these North American nations were in their formative stages when that great volume first appeared and for the following century or two.

One of those who wanted to improve the King James Bible was the American lexicographer Noah Webster. Webster was a great success with his speller, grammar, and reader. His magnum opus, *American Dictionary of the English Language (1828),* was the first English dictionary to give word origins (etymologies). He was also responsible for influencing Americans to adopt a slightly simpler spelling, such as *risk* for *risque.* He also restored the original Latin spelling to *labor, armor, favor,* etc., by dropping the silent "u."

But Webster, a devout Christian, had another project that lasted nearly sixty years, and that was in the area he most cherished—the English Bible. He corrected grammatical errors and replaced obsolete terms in the Authorized Version with contemporary ones.

The nineteenth century was noted for a certain reserve among conservative people. In 1833, to meet the needs of this community Webster published his own edition of the King James Version. He changed all the words and expressions he found "indelicate." They were not merely the sort of words that even today are considered vulgar (see Chapter 8, "Something Blue"), but often expressions that today seem quite harmless.[8]

By giving up his royalties, Webster was able to sell his Bible for only two dollars. Nevertheless Webster's Bible was a failure. Today, even most informed Bible-lovers have never heard of it.

The Accuracy of the King James

The Scottish theologian Alexander Geddes paid the following high tribute to the accuracy and precision of the Authorized (King James) Version of the Holy Bible:

> If accuracy and strictest attention to the letter of the text be supposed to constitute an excellent version, this is of all versions the most accurate.

Now if Geddes had been a member of the Kirk of Scotland, the Free Church, or some such group as the Baptists, this would not be a surprising quotation. But Geddes was a *Roman Catholic* theologian. Moreover he did not live in the modern ecumenical era when it is fashionable for differing religious groups to say nice things about one another. Quite the contrary, Geddes lived in the eighteenth century, a time when Catholics in Great Britain were not especially well treated. In short (as Mr. Micawber in *David Copperfield* would put it), he was "from the enemy camp." Still, he was able to recognize the superiority of the King James tradition.

In recent years it has been common to cast stones at the KJV on the score of accuracy. Let me say, as one who has studied that grand old Bible in the light of the originals at Bible college, seminary, and graduate school, that the King James Version is *very accurate.* The seven years our NKJV teams spent producing the New King James Version kept us delving into its predecessor in minute detail, and always in the light of the Hebrew, Aramaic, and Greek originals.

Our Changing Language

"Why, then," some may ask, "did you not just leave well enough alone and stick with the KJV?" The reason is well known, if not obvious: our language has changed a great deal in nearly 400 years. Things that were accurately rendered in seventeenth-century English may mean something totally different today.

While teaching the Greek text of Romans 5:11 years ago at seminary, I told my third-year class that here we had an example of one of the rare places in the KJV where we had *an actual error.* It reads here "by whom we have now received the *atonement.*" I pointed out that the Greek word there is *katalagē,* which definitely means *reconciliation,* not "atonement."

Later I did some seventeenth-century English study. Encountering the expression "to be at one with" in Shakespeare, I then realized that "at-one-ment" used to mean "reconciliation." The KJV was right, and I was wrong!

I apologized to my Greek class.

Many preachers make even worse mistakes than mine, I fear. Apologies are long overdue for careless assumptions that the KJV is wrong because it doesn't match our current Anglo-American usage.

New Discoveries

Besides changes in English usage, today we know the meanings of some words and expressions, especially in Hebrew, that were just guessed at, or translated from the Septuagint or the Vulgate (sometimes guesses on the part of the ancients!).

While the King James Version is very accurate in the light of its time, we don't believe that the KJV, the NKJV, or indeed *any* translation, is flawless! In the original Introduction the men who translated the KJV tell us in so many words that their work is not perfect. Notwithstanding its many virtues, the version surely needed updating, partly due to the changes in English usage and vocabulary since the seventeenth century, and partly due to new discoveries in archaeology and the original languages. Now, through newly discovered materials in such languages as Ugaritic, we are in a better position to know the exact meaning of certain words.

In the light of these two very important considerations—the many changes in English through the centuries and the new findings in linguistics and archaeology—the need for the New King James was a clear mandate.

NOTES

[1] Miles Smith, Introduction to the original 1611 edition of the Authorized King James.

[2] All were members of the Church of England, but as a state church it contained quite a few varying beliefs.

[3] This story was reported a few years ago by the British Broadcasting Corporation.

[4] F. F. Bruce, *The English Bible: A History of Translations*, p. 99.

[5] Luther A. Weigle, "English Versions Since 1611," *The Cambridge History of the Bible*, p. 361.

[6] It may not still be the most widely *read*, however. For award Bibles, graduation Bibles, bride's Bibles, and gift Bibles for other very traditional events, it has been standard to give the KJV.

[7] It is not always certain which supplied words are clearly implied by the original and which should be considered additions by the translators.

[8] In *Our Marvelous Native Tongue*, Robert Claiborne lists some of Webster's changes, which he obviously considers absurd (p. 174).

3

Rewiring the House

J. B. Phillips described his New Testament translation work as rewiring the house—with the juice on! This illustrates the truth of Hebrews 4:12:

> For the word of God is living and powerful, and sharper than any two-edged sword, piercing even to the division of soul and spirit, and of joints and marrow, and is a discerner of the thoughts and intents of the heart.

Even with the accumulated changes in English through the centuries, millions have been transformed by the spiritual message of the Scriptures in the KJV. Since this is true even when parts of the text are now obscure and sometimes misleading, how much sharper and more powerfully the current will come through if none of the "wires" are frayed and out of date!

The Genesis of the NKJV

Mr. Sam Moore, President of Thomas Nelson Publishers, was deeply concerned that so many Christians, though they devoutly read the King James Bible, do not fully understand it because of its archaic phraseology. This, along with his son Joe's request for a comprehensible Bible, provided the incentive for beginning the work of revising the King James Version. After unsuccessfully approaching several foundations to sponsor this revision, Mr. Moore decided to underwrite the venture himself. He soon realized, however, that this would require a great deal of work under careful control.

Initial Conferences

In order to assure meeting the needs of public worship, Christian education, and personal reading, study, and memorization, Thomas Nelson Publishers determined to consult with informed representatives of the Bible-reading public. So, in 1975, Christian leaders, both men and women, both clergy and laity, were invited to meetings in Chicago, Illinois, Nashville, Tennessee, and London, England, to discuss the need for a revision of the King James Bible. A few of the invited guests were unable to attend any of the meetings, and a small handful of those who did come felt they could not participate in the work. The vast majority of the people who attended either the Chicago or Nashville meeting agreed to become members of the North American Overview Committee.

Mr. Maxey Jarman, a distinguished retired businessman, a Bible-class teacher at First Baptist Church of Nashville for half a century, headed up the North American Committee.

Personal participation depended largely on the time available and level of interest of individual members. It was the old story: "If you want to get something done, ask an already busy person."

A list of the committee members will be found in Appendix C.

The North American Overview Committee

One of the main decisions of all three meetings was that *thee* and *thou* and their accompanying archaic verb forms would not be retained even in poetry and prayer. Two distinguished members who originally opted for *thee*s and *thou*s, at least in prayer, were Dr. Tim LaHaye of California and the Rt. Rev. Goodwin-Hudson, an Anglican bishop from England. At one point the eminent black pastor, E. V. Hill of Los Angeles, rose to his feet and dramatically instructed the convocation that if we had any desire to reach minority groups with this Bible we would have to update the seventeenth-century verb forms and pronouns. His speech helped carry the day. Contemporary pronouns and verb forms, even in poetry and prayer, became the unanimous expression of the Chicago meetings.

The Commonwealth Oversight Committee

A similar convocation was held in England in January 1976. The meetings of this group, smaller and more select than the North American committee, were held at the historic Dorchester Hotel in London.

One of the members was the Rt. Rev. Maurice Wood, Bishop of Norwich and Chaplain to Her Majesty Queen Elizabeth II. Interestingly enough, the one lady invited to attend the London meetings, Mrs. Winifred Gillespie,[1] had known the bishop's family in the 1920s from the Keswick convention. London-born, Oxford- and Toronto-bred Mrs. Gillespie, now a U.S. citizen, made notable contributions to the project, including proofreading the final galleys.

Altogether, the three conferences held in Chicago, Nashville, and London were attended by over one hundred church leaders representing a broad spectrum of biblically oriented Christianity. The consensus of these leaders was that a careful revision of the King James Bible should be made, one that would retain as much as possible of the text and language of that historic version.

By making use of the ideas and suggestions provided at these three conferences, the publishers drafted a statement of purpose and a list of guidelines.

Statement of Purpose

The following is the main body of the Statement of Purpose published by Thomas Nelson in an information brochure:

The purpose of this project is to preserve the original intended purity of the King James Version in its communication of God's Word to man.

Insofar as is humanly and textually possible, the intention is to clarify this translation by the use of current words, grammar, and sentence structure so that this edition of the King James Version will speak to the individual reader in this final quarter of the twentieth century in as clear, simple, and accurate a manner as the original translators of the King James Version in 1611 endeavored to speak to their readers. This edition shall not add to, nor take from, nor alter the communication that was the intent of the original translators.

All participants in this project agree to sign the Statement of Faith that "The Bible (both Old and New Testaments) alone, and the Bible in its entirety (plenary), is the infallible Word of God, and is therefore the inerrant (free from error), inspired (God-breathed) Scripture, in the autographs."

This edition shall not corrupt nor diminish the original translation but shall endeavor to speak in the late twentieth century as simply, clearly, and effectively as possible—all within the format of the original 1611 version— so that a reader of this edition may follow without confusion a reading of the original edition from the pulpit.

Guidelines

A list of instructions was drawn up to guide the scholars and editors who were to do the work. The following are the initial guidelines adopted for use:

The purpose of this project is to produce an updated English Version that follows the sentence structure of the 1611 Authorized Version as closely as possible. As much of the original King James Version as possible will be preserved. The intention is to clarify the 1611 translation by the use of current words, grammar, idioms, and sentence structure so that this edition of the King James Version will speak to the individual reader in a clear and accurate manner. The intention is not to take from or alter the basic communication of the 1611 edition but to transfer the Elizabethan word forms into twentieth-century English.

The traditional texts of the Greek and Hebrew will be used rather than modern critical texts based on the Westcott and Hort theory. Because of the continued popularity of the traditional text (*Textus Receptus*) and the increasing number of scholars who prefer this text because of its support by the majority of manuscripts, it is important that a version of the Bible based on this text be available in current literary English.

In order to accomplish these goals, the following guidelines were followed:

1. Retain all doctrinal and theological words unless the Greek or Hebrew clearly indicates otherwise.

2. Retain words for items no longer in current use (i.e., *chariot* or *phylacteries*).

3. Correct all departures from the Textus Receptus. [See Chapter 10.]

4. Words that have changed meaning since 1611 should be replaced by their modern equivalents.

5. Archaic idioms should be replaced by modern equivalents.

6. Words and expressions that have become vulgar or indelicate in current English usage should be replaced by their proper equivalent. [See Chapter 7.]

7. Alter punctuation to conform with that currently used.

8. Change all Elizabethan pronouns, verb forms, and words having "-eth" endings to their current equivalent.

9. Attempt to keep King James word order. However, when comprehension or readability is affected transpose or revise sentence structure.

10. Eliminate the inordinate usage of the auxiliary verb "shall." Follow current grammatical style for these changes.

11. Attempt to keep sentences reasonably short without affecting text or meaning.

12. Attempt to use words that avoid misunderstanding.

13. When making corrections use other words already represented by the same Greek or Hebrew word in the King James if possible.

14. Capitalize all personal pronouns referring to deity.

15. Proper names should agree with Old Testament when possible.

16. All obsolete and archaic words as defined by one or more recognized dictionaries should be replaced by their current equivalents. This applies to phrases and idioms as well.

In addition, after the printing of the first edition of the NKJV New Testament in 1979 (which used no italics), the King James tradition of italicizing supplied words was restored by popular demand of the readers. (See Chapter 4, "Italics.")

Obsolete and Archaic Words

It is possible to overemphasize the archaic material in the KJV. The fact that millions still read it every day would indicate that much of it is still at least largely understandable. On the other hand, the Old Testament especially does use some words and expressions that are puzzling at best to most readers.

A person meeting the words *ouches* or *firkins* could always look them up. (Few do, however, and most dictionaries don't list obsolete words.)

A greater problem is those *words that are still used but have changed their meanings.*

A second category consists of words that are archaic only in certain meanings, such as the following:

apt	when it means	"able"
charity	when it means	"love"
communicate	when it means	"share"
conversation	when it means	"conduct" or "citizenship"
exceeding	when used as:	an adverb (i.e. "exceeding wise")
except	when it means	"unless"
issue	when it means	"flow" or "discharge"

35

meat	when it means	"food"
mine	when it means	"my"
press	when it means	"crowd"
put away	when it means	"divorce"
quick or quickened	when it means	"alive"
room	when it means	"place"
save	when it means	"but," "only," or "but only"
scarce	when used as:	an adverb (i.e. "scarce perceive")
several	when it means	"individual"
singleness	when it means	"sincerity"
sore	when it means	"very"
space	when it refers to:	a time concept
strange	when it means	"foreign"
stranger	when it means	"foreigner"
straw	when it means	"scatter"
suffer	when it means	"let" or "allow"
table	when it means	"tablet"
touching	when it means	"concerning"
tribute	when it means	"tax"
wax	when it means	"grow" or "become"

The NKJV Philosophy: Proven Tradition

Rather than trying to start a "new tradition," the philosophy behind the New King James Version is that of the *proven* tradition which began in 1526 with the linguistic genius William Tyndale.

The Initial Translations

Translators excelling in the original languages from all segments of conservative Christianity from all over the English-speaking world were enlisted for the first phase—the revision of individual books. In order to encourage adherence to the KJV text as much as possible, the very first draft was actually made on enlarged, giant-print pages of the King James Bible.

Translators were chosen for books partly according to their interest and special training. For example, the late Dr. E. M. Blaiklock of New Zealand, a classical scholar, revised the Book of Acts. After receiving my comments on his revision of chapters one and two, this fine scholar completed the book, adhering so closely to the guidelines that there was little work for the New Testament editor to do.

For a list of these translators see Appendix A.

The Editorial Phase

Needless to say, not all translators were as close to the mark as Dr. Blaiklock. Some scholars made too few changes, leaving some archaic or borderline expressions.

One or two revisers deviated too far from the King James translation. One New Testament Epistle was very easy to read and nicely done, but was far removed from the traditional phrasing. These deviations from the guidelines were corrected in subsequent editing.

On the whole the revisers' work was outstanding, not surprisingly, in light of the caliber of scholars chosen.

It was a joy and privilege for the three main Editors—Dr. William McDowell, Dr. James Price, and myself—to spend hours every day interacting with these typescripts.[2]

In some cases, especially in the Old Testament, the work was reviewed by an editorial assistant who did the preliminary work. This consisted of reviewing the manuscript, marking the places requiring attention, and providing helpful notes, data, and suggestions for the Executive Editor.

The advice of experts and consultants was obtained to resolve difficult problems. For example, when "goodly pearls" was to be updated, we called a jeweler to see what he would call them. In revising the sections in Leviticus regarding parts of animals, Dr. Price conferred with veterinarians and other experts. (See Appendix A for a list of Consultants.)

The English Editing Phase

All edited typescripts were carefully reviewed by our English Editor, Dr. William McDowell, who made the necessary corrections and revisions associated with English grammar and style. Strict attention was given to maintaining the standard of literary excellence of the King James tradition. McDowell worked closely with Dr. Price and myself to make sure all changes conformed to the original languages.[3] The Bible Editorial Department of Thomas Nelson prepared the revised typescripts.

The Early Review Phase

The revised typescript of each book was sent to several reviewers. A copy was sent to the initial translator and several other scholars. In addition a copy was sent to several members of the Overview and Oversight Committees, and to other reviewers and consultants. These reviewers provided practical and scholarly comments and suggestions. All comments and suggestions were carefully reviewed by the Old and New Testament Editors for discussion with the Executive Review Committee.

When this review phase was over, we thought it was time to proceed with publication. But President Moore decided to establish what he called an "Executive Review Committee" for each Testament. Each committee would go over every verse again to ensure uniformity of treatment, accuracy, and acceptability by the public.

The Executive Review Phase

Mr. Moore proved to be right. The efforts of the Executive Review Committee (ERC) greatly enhanced the quality of the finished product. The many long meetings and the delay in publication were well worth the added investment of time and finances.

The combination of the months spent with a laymen's group, led by Mr. Maxey Jarman in early days, and with the ERC in the last years of the work, stretched out the preparation of the Bible to seven years (1975–1982)— coincidentally as much time as was taken to prepare the first King James Version (1604–1611).

The Executive Review Committees, under the leadership of the Old and New Testament Executive Editors and the English Editor, met periodically to consider the suggested changes made by the reviewers. Meetings often lasted a week or two, and were held in a number of North American cities, including Nashville, Toronto, San Diego, Chattanooga, and Ft. Worth. Strict attention was given to maintaining the guidelines and good literary standards. Each suggested change was carefully considered, and the decision of the committee determined the final form of the text. Dr. McDowell was present in the committee meetings and gave judgment on all matters of grammar and style. Any changes in the text following the committee's deliberations were approved by the committee in subsequent sessions.

The New Testament Executive Review Committee

It was my privilege to chair this committee at every meeting except one.[4] On that occasion Dr. Harry Sturz of Biola was chairman *pro tem.*

The other members of the New Testament ERC were Dr. Robert Hughes, Dr. Alfred Martin, Dr. Robert Reymond, and Dr. Curtis Vaughan.

Dr. William McDowell, our very experienced English stylist and editor from Canada,[5] was also active on this committee in keeping "Hellenistic English" out of the final typescript! See Appendix B for the scholars' credentials.

As we worked around large tables with lexicons, ancient versions, and modern translations opened to the passage under review, the hours, days, and years passed quickly and without harsh disputes. All were persuaded that we had divine direction in the work. Each session was opened with prayer for wisdom.

The Old Testament Executive Review Committee

The executive review sessions for the New Testament were completed in 1978. At that point I was asked to join the sessions of the Old Testament ERC. These began in 1979 and were concluded in 1981. The final session of the Old Testament Executive Review Committee was held at St. Andrews University, in St. Andrews, Scotland, during the month of July.

Beginning in 1979, the year the New Testament was published, James D. Price, who holds degrees from both evangelical (Los Angeles Baptist Seminary) and Jewish (Dropsie College for Hebrew and Cognate Learning, Philadelphia) institutions, led the Old Testament scholars with dignity and expertise. His encyclopedic knowledge of the Hebrew text, vocabulary, and syntax were impressive.

Again, Dr. McDowell persisted in encouraging the use of standard English, rather than "Anglo-Semitic."

The other members of the Old Testament ERC were Dr. David Garland, Dr. Herbert Livingston, Dr. Paul Gilchrist, Dr. Roland K. Harrison, and myself. See Appendix B for these scholars' credentials.

After the New Testament ERC finished its deliberations in 1978, I was appointed Executive Editor of the Bible project as a whole.

Thus it was my privilege to attend all meetings of both Executive Review Committees, except for the last week in Scotland when the two committees met separately and simultaneously. For those meetings I chaired the New Testament group again, which was a nostalgic experience after three years of no New Testament meetings.

The Scottish Sessions

During our month at St. Andrews University, Thomas Nelson Publishers treated us to an historic and delightful weekend holiday through the lovely Lake District in the North of England. We visited Durham Cathedral, the burial site of the renowned church historian, the Venerable Bede.[6] We also spent the night in an English castle, and on the way back to St. Andrews we visited Bobbie Burns's cottage and monument.

Some of us visited Stirling Castle in Scotland, the birthplace of King James himself. Bill McDowell and I, both admirers of the revered Scottish saint, Robert Murray M'Cheyne (1813–1843), made a pilgrimage to his church and tomb at Dundee. On the way home we missed the bus. As night fell we sat on a bench as I read one of M'Cheyne's sermons to Bill. It was a spiritual high point of our Scottish adventure.

Anglo-American Cooperation

The Old Testament Committee held a joint meeting with some of the members of the British Oversight Committee on Thursday, July 23, 1981. Those British members present were: the Rev. Mr. Raymond Brown, Mr. Edward England, Mr. David K. Porter, Sir J. Eric Richardson, the Rev. Mr. David Wheaton, and Mr. William J. Cameron. The progress of the project was reviewed, and there was a profitable exchange of ideas. In the afternoon the Executive Review Committee sat in session with the British scholars participating. Sir Eric Richardson, who had recently been knighted by the Queen, was especially interested to see how we were handling the concept of leprosy, especially in the Old Testament. Dr. R. K. Harrison, who also has a strong medical background, assured him that we would have suitable explanatory footnotes in the Old Testament on this difficult issue.

During the last week of July the New Testament Committee also met in St. Andrews to consider proposed changes to the New Testament text and to meet in joint session with the Old Testament Committee. Numerous improvements to the New Testament were approved.

The Old Testament Committee finished work on the Book of Malachi at 9:45 A.M. on Tuesday, July 28. Members of the New Testament Committee, along with some of the wives, were present to witness the finale. When the last verse was completed, we all rose and sang the Doxology. Our beloved coordinator, Rev. Robert Sanford of Thomas Nelson, Nashville, his voice broken with emotion, led us in prayer, followed by prayers by Dr. Price, Dr. McDowell, and myself. This was a time of great rejoicing and praise to God. The rest of the day was spent resolving technical problems held from previous meetings.

The work on the Old Testament as a whole officially ended on Wednesday, July 29, 1981, the day of the wedding of Prince Charles and Lady Diana. On that day work began at 6:30 A.M., but we took a break from 10:25 A.M. to 1:30 P.M. to watch the royal wedding on television, thus joining the British Commonwealth and its people in their celebration. We were pleased that the service used the Authorized Version. By unanimous vote of the committee, our work on the complete Bible officially ended at 6:00 P.M. on Thursday, July 30, when the Old Testament Committee met in joint session with the New Testament Committee.

Typesetting and Printing Phase

Typesetting and production of the Bibles, performed by means of the most advanced computer technology, was coordinated by the Bible Editorial Department of Thomas Nelson. Typesetting was begun as soon as the Pentateuch had passed through the hands of the Executive Review Committee. Succeeding blocks of text were typeset as the committee work was completed. The Executive Editors and English Editor assisted in reading the galleys. There were thirteen proofreaders of the New Testament. The last proofreader, Mrs. Gillespie, found the pronoun "He" capitalized where it referred, not to the Deity, but to Herod!

The first edition of the New Testament was issued in 1979. The next production was the New Testament with Psalms, published in 1980. The complete Bible appeared on August 2, 1982. Interestingly, this was six hundred years after John Wycliffe issued the first English Bible in 1382.

NOTES

[1]Mrs. Gillespie is the daughter of the well-known Anglican scholar and Bible-teacher, W. H. Griffith Thomas. Dr. Thomas was principal of Wycliffe Hall, Oxford, later professor of Old Testament at Wycliffe College, Toronto, and one of the founders of Dallas Theological Seminary in 1924.

[2]During much of this laborious yet joyous time in my life, my office was located in my home. Each day as I worked there on the NKJV, the manuscripts were guarded and even occasionally "autographed" with paw prints by my faithful canine companion, Mr. Chips (named for the character in the classic English book and film, *Goodbye Mr. Chips*).

[3]We were fortunate in that our English Editor also had been through the disciplines of Hebrew and Greek at Westminster Seminary.

[4]During the seven-year project I had my gall bladder removed in 1978 and quadruple bypass surgery in 1980.

[5]Dr. McDowell hails from Windsor, Nova Scotia and studied in Toronto, Philadelphia, and Orlando.

[6]While a senior at seminary I did an oil painting of the interior of this great Norman cathedral, based on an old woodcut, so it was a thrill to see that interior in the actual colors.

4

Finishing Touches

Dr. Helen Smith passed out the Sunday School folders for coloring by her 1940s primary class. Tow-headed Arthur, recently transferred from a Yonkers Sunday School to this little class meeting in Washington's Georgetown area, was thrilled. The cover featured an outline picture of King Solomon, sitting on a pier, watching his cargo being unloaded from his ships of Tarshish: ivory, apes, and peacocks. *Peacocks!* Great for a crayola kid. Think of how many colors you could use!

Little did young Arthur realize that decades later he would help "unload" the peacocks from Solomon's cargo once and for all. You see, the Hebrew word[1] translated *peacocks* is now known to refer to animals of the simian variety—baboons (NIV) or monkeys (NKJV). Accuracy demands we keep up with the latest findings—at least where they're certain.

In this respect Lord Chesterfield's lines are appropriate:

"Be not the first by whom the new is tried,
Nor yet the last to lay the old aside."

It is possible for Bible scholars and translators to accept too readily the findings (and sometimes mere theories!) in the learned journals. Just because it's new doesn't mean it's necessarily true.

The other extreme is perhaps just as bad—being the last to lay aside a rendering that has been generally shown to be incorrect.

The NKJV, as usual, has taken a balanced but conservative position, somewhere between these extremes.

In our previous chapter we traced the general process by which the King James Version became the New King James Version.

In this, our final chapter on accuracy, we would like to review briefly some of the finishing touches that went into the new version, both before and after the NKJV was published.

As mentioned before, archaeology and the study of languages cognate to Hebrew have revealed the true meanings of a number of Hebrew and fewer Greek words—words that were previously translated by good guessing from the context. Unfortunately, when the mystery word is a noun describing an unknown object, the context often is not a safe guide.

43

Besides the peacock/monkey illustration, we will present some interesting examples of other problem words.

Old Testament Examples

We have chosen three sample revisions from the many that could be cited from the Hebrew Old Testament.

Kill / Murder—Exodus 20:13

Thou shalt not <u>kill</u> (KJV).   You shall not <u>murder</u> (NKJV).

The son of a very strict minister from one of the smaller Baptist denominations was explaining why he had not followed his father's teachings. He said that the Bible had contradictions, such as allowing capital punishment (which he opposed) and yet the *sixth* commandment said, "Thou shalt not kill." I explained to him that Hebrew had two separate verbs[2] here, and that the commandment literally means, "You shall not murder," quite a different thing from executions by the recognized government after due process of law. Actually, this change in the NKJV is not a new find. The Douai Bible said centuries ago, "Thou shalt do no murder," a very good translation for its time. But the change in the King James tradition was long overdue and very important.

File / Pim—1 Samuel 13:21

Yet they had a <u>file</u> for the mattocks, and for the coulters, and for the axes, and to sharpen the goads (KJV).	And the charge for a sharpening was a <u>pim</u>[3] for the plowshares, the mattocks, the forks, and the axes, and to set the points of the goads (NKJV).

This verse shows how not knowing a little technical term can obscure the meaning of a text. It also illustrates other archaic expressions that no longer mean much except to experts in seventeenth-century usage.

Linen Yarn / Keveh—1 Kings 10:28; 2 Chronicles 1:16

And Solomon had horses brought out of Egypt, and linen yarn: the king's merchants received the linen yarn at a price (KJV).

Also Solomon had horses imported from Egypt and Keveh; the king's merchants bought them in Keveh at the current price (NKJV).

The "linen yarn" of the KJV does not even seem to be a very good guess in the context of horse trading. We now know that Keveh was a place noted for horse-breeding.

New Testament Examples

Contention, Strife / Selfish Ambition—Philippians 1:16; cf. 2:3

The Greek word *eritheia* was once thought to be related to *eris,* "strife," and translated accordingly. Both words appear in lists of sins in 2 Corinthians 12:20 and Galatians 5:20, which of course gives it little or no "context," but does suggest that they would not both mean "strife" or "contention." The contexts of both Philippians 1:16 and of 2:3 favor a meaning like "selfish ambition":

The one preach Christ even of contention, not sincerely, supposing to add affliction to my bonds (KJV).

The former preach Christ from selfish ambition, not sincerely, supposing to add affliction to my chains (NKJV).

The older rendering cannot be said to be definitely wrong, but the newer one is better, especially in context.[4]

Taxed, Taxing / Registered, Census—Luke 2:1, 2

Every Christmas Eve our family would read Luke 2 by the light of the Christmas tree. Doubtless millions of other families have a similar tradition. For this reason it is hard to change even a word of the Christmas story, so deeply is it imbedded in our hearts. Yet in the very first two verses there are two words in the KJV that are not quite correct:

And it came to pass in those days, that there went out a decree from Caesar Augustus, that all the world

And it came to pass in those days that a decree went out from Caesar Augustus that all the world

should be <u>taxed.</u> 2 (And this <u>taxing</u> was first made when Cyrenius was governor of Syria) (KJV).	should be <u>registered.</u> 2 This <u>census</u> first took place while Quirinius was governing Syria (NKJV).

Joseph, Mary, and the rest of the Roman Empire were not going up to be *taxed*—not yet at least! They were going because their names had to be registered in a census. A government cannot tax the people unless it has first recorded them on its tax rolls. As devout Jews submissive to the authorities, Joseph and Mary heeded the decree—and thereby unknowingly fulfilled Micah 5:2 by going all the way to Bethlehem.

The Definite Article

English, unlike Latin which lacks it, has a full use of the definite article *the,* similar to Greek usage. The Greek article is more sophisticated and varied in its usage no doubt, but frequently the two languages match. This is an area where the King James needed some improvement. There are places where the Greek has the definite article and the English would be clearer with it as well. Romans 5:15 is an example:

15 But not as the offence, so also is the free gift. For if through the offence of one many be dead, much more the grace of God, and the gift of grace, which is by one man, Jesus Christ, hath abounded unto many (KJV).	15 But the free gift is not like the offense. For if by <u>the</u> one man's offense many died, much more the grace of God and the gift by the grace of <u>the</u> one Man, Jesus Christ, abounded to many (NKJV).

The definite article makes the translation precisely accurate.

An area where English does *not* match Greek is in the so-called "generic use of the article." This means that when talking about a category, such as types of animals, people, or things, Greek uses the article and English tends not to. This is shown in Matthew 8:20:

<u>The</u> foxes have holes, and <u>the</u> birds of the air have nests; (KJV).	Foxes have holes and birds of the air have nests, (NKJV).

It is more idiomatic not to use an article in English in such a situation, since for us the article tends to point out specific objects, not classes.

The Consistency Check

It is well known that the King James translators were fond of translating the same Greek word several different ways in one passage for literary variety. They also would sometimes translate different Greek or Hebrew words with the same English word. If all of these were to be computerized so that the same Greek word was always translated the same way, it would not be the King James tradition. Neither would it be good English style!

However, most careful students of the Scriptures felt that the 1611 "learned men" overdid the variety motif. For this reason a detailed and laborious "consistency check" was performed, using the fine *Greek-English Concordance* of the Mennonite scholar, J. B. Smith. This volume presents the KJV translations of Greek words in chart form. The New King James is much more consistent than the Old, but without going overboard on changes.

For example, in parallel passages, if a certain word was translated "garment" in one Gospel, "vesture" in another, "raiment" in a third, and "clothing" in a fourth, the two archaic words would be changed to the same word as one of the others. There would then be two, not four, translations of this word.

On the other side of the coin, in John 13, two very different Greek verbs are both translated "wash" in the KJV.[5] Here the symbolic argument of the footwashing versus the complete bath is lost in the older version. "Bathe" is the correct rendering for the body, "wash" for the feet.

Juggling Potatoes

A sergeant assigned a buck private to sort potatoes as his "K.P." (Kitchen Police) duty.

"Put the big potatoes in one pile and the small ones in another pile."

Coming back some time later, the sergeant was angry to see that the private couldn't even carry out so simple an order. There were not two, but *three* stacks of potatoes.

"Hey, what's the big idea, Sonny? What is that third pile all about?"

"Oh, Sarge," the private explained brightly, "those are the potatoes that were too little to put in the pile of big potatoes and too big to put in the pile of little ones!"

In working on the New King James Version we had a similar problem: "borderline potatoes." It would have actually been easier and less work to start a new translation from scratch. Then we would only have had to deal with two clear-cut issues: the original text and modern usage. Juggling two "potatoes" is not so hard. However, a careful revision has a third item to juggle: those borderline readings of the older version that were slightly old but probably still have some mileage.

Clearly archaic, obsolete, or even vulgar expressions were no problem. They had to go!

The Nashville Convocation

For some strange reason, no matter how many people of all walks of life read and interact with typescripts, only after a Bible is actually published do certain little problems surface. The RSV and the NIV—not to mention the original KJV—shared this same experience.[6]

Because this is so, after the NKJV had been in print for about two years, Mr. Moore called a convocation of Christian leaders as well as a group of translators to Nashville.

On August 13th and 14th of 1984, the convocation was held at the beautiful Opryland Hotel.

Two distinguished new translators were invited to join the original teams—Dr. James Borland of Liberty University and Professor Zane C. Hodges, then of Dallas Theological Seminary. Although Hodges was not a translator of any New Testament book, I consulted him on several knotty problems during the days of editing the New Testament.

The participants in the larger group included several men and women whose names are household words in their own disciplines, and some who are well known in Christian circles generally.

Dr. Charles C. Ryrie[7] gave a fascinating lecture on the Geneva Bible as an example of which aspects of a version make for wide popularity.

Other well-known Christians at the convocation included Dr. Bill Bright of Campus Crusade for Christ, Dr. Jack Wyrtzen, evangelist and head of Word of Life, and Dr. Charles Stanley, at that time President of the Southern Baptist Convention.

Although Dr. Thomas Zimmerman, General Overseer of the Assemblies of God, was unable to attend, Mrs. Juleen Turnage, the Secretary of Information, came to represent him and their denomination. She made very valuable contributions to the discussion. Other women who contributed their wisdom were author and lecturer Mrs. Jill Briscoe, and Evelyn Christenson, President of United Prayer Ministries, whose book *What Happens When Women Pray?* has been very popular.

The entire list of delegates, all outstanding people in their own right, will be found in Appendix D.

In consultation with the Christian leaders, the primary goal of the Translation Committee was to improve the NKJV with enhancements of

English vocabulary and style, smoother use of connectives, and more consistency between parallel passages.

The Finished Product: Selected Comparisons

A very wise old Anglo-Saxon saying is, "The proof of the pudding is in the tasting." This applies to Bible Versions as well as puddings. The quality of *accuracy* and the character of the New King James Version may be appreciated by sampling the dual passages presented below. Underlining is added to highlight key revisions. Several more passages illustrating literary *beauty* will be found in the second main section of our book.

1 Thessalonians 4:13-18

KJV	NKJV
13 But I would not have you to be ignorant, brethren, concerning them which <u>are asleep</u>, that ye sorrow not, even as others which have no hope.	13 But I do not want you to be ignorant, brethren, concerning those who <u>have fallen asleep</u>, lest you sorrow as others who have no hope.
14 For if we believe that Jesus died and rose again, even so them also which sleep in Jesus will God bring with him.	14 For if we believe that Jesus died and rose again, even so God will bring with Him those who sleep in Jesus.
15 For this we say unto you by the word of the Lord, that we which are alive and remain unto the coming of the Lord shall not <u>prevent</u> them which are asleep.	15 For this we say to you by the word of the Lord, that we who are alive and remain until the coming of the Lord will by no means <u>precede</u> those who are asleep.
16 For the Lord himself shall descend from heaven with a shout, with the voice of the archangel, and with the <u>trump</u> of God: and the dead in Christ shall rise first:	16 For the Lord Himself will descend from heaven with a shout, with the voice of an archangel, and with the <u>trumpet</u> of God. And the dead in Christ will rise first.
17 Then we which are alive and remain shall be caught up together with them in the clouds, to meet the Lord in the air: and so shall we <u>ever</u> be with the Lord.	17 Then we who are alive and remain shall be caught up together with them in the clouds to meet the Lord in the air. And thus we shall <u>always</u> be with the Lord.
18 <u>Wherefore</u> comfort one another with these words.	18 <u>Therefore</u> comfort one another with these words.

This passage illustrates those texts that needed very little change. However, verse 15 does contain a most interesting example of a word (*prevent*) that has almost done a complete 180-degree change in meaning. A person reading the KJV would likely get a totally false picture of what Paul meant.

Isaiah 19:5-10

KJV	NKJV
5 And the waters shall fail from the sea, and the river shall be wasted and dried up.	5 The waters will fail from the sea, And the river will be wasted and dried up.
6 And they shall turn the rivers <u>far away</u>; and the brooks of defence shall be emptied and dried up: the reeds and <u>flags</u> shall wither.	6 The rivers will turn <u>foul</u>, And the brooks of defense will be emptied and dried up; The reeds and <u>rushes</u> will wither.
7 The <u>paper</u> reeds by the <u>brooks</u>, by the mouth of the <u>brooks</u>, and every thing sown by the <u>brooks</u>, shall wither, be driven away, and be no more.	7 The <u>papyrus</u> reeds by the <u>River</u>, by the mouth of the <u>River</u>, And everything sown by the <u>River</u>, Will wither, be driven away, and be no more.
8 The fishers also shall mourn, and all they that cast <u>angle</u> into the <u>brooks</u> shall lament, and they that spread nets upon the waters shall languish.	8 The fishermen also will mourn; All those will lament who cast <u>hooks</u> into the <u>River</u>, And they will languish who spread nets on the waters.
9 Moreover they that work in fine flax, and they that weave <u>networks</u>, shall be confounded.	9 Moreover those who work in fine flax, And those who weave <u>fine fabric</u> will be ashamed;
10 And they shall be broken in the <u>purposes</u> thereof, all that make <u>sluices and ponds for fish.</u>	10 And <u>its foundations</u> will be broken. All who make <u>wages</u> will be <u>troubled of soul.</u>

The changes in the interest of accuracy here are *papyrus* for paper (verse 7), *hooks* for angle, and replacing the very odd translation *"fish"* in verse 10 with *soul,* the usual translation of the Hebrew word. Here the KJV was following the Vulgate.

Jeremiah 10:21-22

KJV	NKJV
21 For the <u>pastors</u> are become <u>brutish</u>, and have not sought the	21 For the <u>shepherds</u> have become <u>dull-hearted,</u>

LORD: therefore they shall not prosper, and all their flocks shall be scattered.
22 Behold, the noise of the <u>bruit</u> is come, and a great commotion out of the north country, to make the cities of Judah desolate, and a den of <u>dragons</u>.

And have not sought the LORD; Therefore they shall not prosper, And all their flocks shall be scattered.
22 Behold, the noise of the <u>report</u> has come,
And a great commotion out of the north country,
To make the cities of Judah desolate, a den of <u>jackals</u>.

Pastors is Latin for *shepherds,* but in English the word today suggests a local church situation. Other words that needed updating are *brutish, bruit,* and the non-existent *dragons!*

Ezekiel 41:7

KJV

7 And there was an enlarging, and a winding about still upward to the side chambers: for the winding about of the house went still upward round about the house: therefore the breadth of the house was still upward, and so increased from the lowest chamber to the highest by the midst.

NKJV

7 As one went up from story to story, the side chambers became wider all around, because their supporting ledges in the wall of the temple ascended like steps; therefore the width of the structure increased as one went up from the lowest story to the highest by way of the middle one.

I call this "the most expensive verse in the NKJV." No underlining is used because nearly all of both verses would have to be underlined to show the clarifications. Eight of us spent all morning in the Williamsburg Room of Southwestern Baptist Theological Seminary working on this one verse to make it comprehensible. Architecture without blueprints is very difficult! An attorney friend of mine likes the KJV rendering because, as he put it, "It's mystical." He admitted, however, that he had absolutely no idea what it means!

Acts 27:13-27

KJV	NKJV

KJV

13 And when the south wind blew softly, supposing that they had obtained their purpose, <u>loosing thence</u>, they sailed close by Crete.
14 But not long after there arose against it a <u>tempestuous wind</u>, called Euroclydon.
15 And when the ship was caught, and could not <u>bear up into the wind</u>, we let here drive.
16 And running <u>under</u> a certain island which is called Clauda, we <u>had much work to come by the boat</u>:
17 Which when they had <u>taken up</u>, they <u>used helps</u>, undergirding the ship; and, fearing lest they should <u>fall into the quicksands, strake sail</u>, and so were driven.
18 And we being exceedingly tossed with a tempest, the next day they lightened the ship;
19 And the third day we cast out with our own hands the <u>tackling</u> of the ship.
20 And when neither sun nor stars in many days appeared, and no small tempest lay on us, all hope that we should be saved was then taken away.
21 But after long <u>abstinence</u> Paul stood forth in the midst of them, and said, Sirs, ye should have hearkened unto me, and not have <u>loosed</u> from Crete, and to have <u>gained</u> this harm and loss.
22 And now I <u>exhort</u> you to be of good cheer: for there shall be no loss of any man's life among you, but of the ship.
23 For there stood by me this night the angel of God, whose I am, and whom I serve,

NKJV

13 When the south wind blew softly, supposing that they had obtained their purpose, <u>putting out to sea</u>, they sailed close by Crete.
14 But not long after, a tempestuous <u>head wind</u> arose, called Euroclydon.
15 So when the ship was caught, and could not <u>head into the wind</u>, we let her drive.
16 And running under <u>the shelter of</u> an island called Clauda, <u>we secured the skiff with difficulty</u>.
17 When they had <u>taken it on board</u>, they <u>used cables</u> to undergird the ship; and fearing lest they should <u>run aground on the Syrtis Sands</u>, they <u>struck sail</u> and so were driven.
18 And because we were exceedingly tempest-tossed, the next day they lightened the ship.
19 On the third day we threw the ship's <u>tackle</u> overboard with our own hands.
20 Now when neither sun nor stars appeared for many days, and no small tempest beat on us, all hope that we would be saved was finally given up.
21 But after long <u>abstinence from food</u>, then Paul stood in the midst of them and said, "Men, you should have listened to me, and not have <u>sailed</u> from Crete and <u>incurred</u> this disaster and loss.
22 "And now I <u>urge</u> you to take heart, for there will be no loss of life among you, but only of the ship.
23 "For there stood by me this night an angel of the God to whom I belong and whom I serve,

24 Saying, Fear not, Paul; thou must be brought before Caesar: and, <u>lo</u>, God hath given thee all them that sail with thee.
25 Wherefore, sirs, <u>be of good cheer</u>: for I believe God, that it shall be even as it was told me.
26 Howbeit we must <u>be cast upon</u> a certain island.
27 But when the fourteenth night was come, as we were driven up and down in <u>Adria</u>, about midnight the <u>shipmen</u> deemed that they drew near to some *country.*

24 "saying, 'Do not be afraid, Paul; you must be brought before Caesar; and <u>indeed</u> God has granted you all those who sail with you.'
25 "Therefore <u>take heart</u>, men, for I believe God that it will be just as it was told me.
26 "However, we must <u>run aground</u> on a certain island."
27 But when the fourteenth night had come, as we were driven up and down in <u>the Adriatic Sea</u>, about midnight the <u>sailors</u> sensed that they were drawing near some *land.*

This exciting shipwreck chapter is full of nautical terms. Unfortunately, most of them in the KJV are no longer used. The changes are many and necessary. We have underscored them in both texts to facilitate comparison.

Use of Italics

Most lovers of the King James Bible know that the italicized words denote language that is not in the original Greek or Hebrew, but which is supplied by the translators to complete the sense of an English sentence. These words have always been a problem to editors because it is often hard to determine whether certain words should be considered as part of a word in the original or italicized as a supplied word. Most places, however, are clear.

In 1979, when the New Testament was published in the New King James Version, the editors and publisher agreed to do away with italics for two reasons. First was the problem mentioned above as to exactly which words should be italicized. A second problem is that today italics usually mean emphasis (or a foreign word). Occasionally, even preachers will not know the KJV tradition and emphasize the very words that have no specific words behind them in the original!

On this issue the public spoke out in no uncertain terms: "Restore the italics!" Many people feel safer with a translation if they are able to tell where the words have been added.

Two other small items of accuracy regarding italics: First, italics have been used more consistently in the New King James Version to reflect the structure and meaning of the original text. Also, some italicized words that were formerly in the King James Bible are omitted in the New King James because they are no longer needed to complete the English sense.

This chapter illustrates the minute but severe language problems that confront translation committees, particularly when revising a centuries-old English Bible. The best of both worlds—the ancient and the modern—must be maintained.

NOTES

[1]The word *tukkîîm* occurs only in 1 Kings 10:22 and the parallel passage in 2 Chronicles 9:21. Koehler-Baumgartner list "Affe/ape" as a translation in *Lexicon in Veteris Testamenti Libros,* p. 1028.

[2]"Kill" is *qātal* and "murder" is *rātzah.*

[3]NKJV note: "About two-thirds shekel weight."

[4]See Arndt, Gingrich, and Danker, *A Greek-English Lexicon of the New Testament and Other Early Christian Literature,* p. 309.

[5]"Wash" is *niptō* and "bathe" is *louō.*

[6]For example, the RSV vacillated between *consecrate* and *sanctify* in John 17 in early printings.

[7]Dr. Ryrie, former Chairman of the Department of Systematic Theology at Dallas Seminary, has authored a host of widely-read books. The *Ryrie Study Bible* is available in the NKJV (Moody Press).

PART TWO:

Beauty

"He has made everything beautiful in its time" (Ecclesiastes 3:11a).

Beautiful brides in English-speaking countries have traditionally worn—

"Something old,
Something new,
Something borrowed,
Something blue."

These four items form a pleasing analogy to the four things that the translators and editors of the NKJV sought to retain and even enhance in wedding the Tyndale—King James tradition to today's usage. The four chapters of this second section, Beauty, will follow the order of the saying:

5. Something Old — The ancient beauties from the original up through the Vulgate, and how very much is still enshrined in the KJV/NKJV.

6. Something New — The fresh modernizations of language, punctuation, and format that improve the beauty of the Bible for today's readers.

7. Something Borrowed — The justly celebrated and beautiful texts that have been borrowed from the KJV almost unchanged because of their familiarity and cadence.

8. Something Blue — The change from some expressions that many consider vulgar or "blue" language to currently acceptable expressions that are "true blue."

5

Something Old

A charming old Scandinavian custom calls for the bride to wear a crown atop her head on her wedding day. Some of these cherished ornaments are very old and are passed on from mother to daughter with each successive generation of brides. This chapter seeks to address the "crown" of good translation, describing the beautiful elements that are enjoyed by ever new generations of Bible readers of various backgrounds. The Church, which the New Testament calls the Bride of Christ, likewise should pass on to succeeding generations not only the truth, but also the beauty of her biblical heritage to her spiritual daughters (and sons).

In the first chapter of this section of our book we propose to consider the *beauty* found in the King James tradition that is so old that it predates the 1611 King James Version itself.

First of all, though, we must answer the question, "What is beauty?" No easy answer presents itself. As the Scottish lady put it, "It's better felt than telt!"

"Beauty," my father used to say, "is in the eye of the beholder." He was no doubt at least partly right. Our tastes in clothing, architecture, music, art, male or female attractiveness, are somewhat conditioned by cultural and ethnic background. Nevertheless, there are some things that seem to be accepted as *universally beautiful.*

Who does not thrill to a gorgeous glowing sunset, a burst of bluebonnets[1] bedecking a hillside, the crashing waves of the sea against the shore, a sparkling snowscape, majestic purple mountains?

In the area of living creatures, who does not admire the grace of an Olympic athlete, the multi-colored plumage of a tropical bird, and the lovely markings on an exotic fish?

In the untold thousands of English-speaking churches—and that includes people from all the racial groups in the world (not merely European, but also African and Asian)—the vast majority of Bible-readers and Bible-lovers who have properly been exposed to the Authorized or King James Version have thrilled to the matchless cadences of the Psalms, the Song of Songs, the rhapsodies of Isaiah, the Beatitudes, 1 Corinthians 13, and the songs in Revelation—to mention just a few. What is the origin of this beauty?

To hear some people talk one would think that Bible translators, especially those who did pioneer work in earlier days, pulled together some diverse and poorly written materials, and by dint of their own outstanding creativity produced "the Bible."

Actually, most of the beauties of the Holy Bible are much deeper and older than any translation or famous version. In fact, we could call this chapter "Something Ancient" and not be wide of the mark.

Beauties from the Original

Dr. Milton C. Fisher of the Reformed Episcopal Seminary of Philadelphia, himself an accomplished communicator, agrees with that modern master of English style C. S. Lewis[2] that most of the beautiful impact of the Authorized (King James) Version is really that of the contents of the Bible itself. Fisher writes:

> Our aesthetic experience or reactions to reading stories from the Old and New Testaments depends very little upon the artistry of the translator. It is to the original text that the King James Version owes much of its "style"—its narrative power, its images and figures.[3]

The same can be said for the New King James in its retention of most of the beauty that still communicates in the end of the twentieth and dawn of the twenty-first centuries. (See Chapter 7, "Something Borrowed," for this fascinating theme.)

The truth of Lewis's and Fisher's contention can be appreciated by those who have gained enough proficiency in Hebrew or Greek—or both—to *enjoy* reading the original texts. Others will have to accept this teaching by faith!

Since God is Himself the fountainhead of creativity and beauty, we should not be surprised that His Word is a reflection of that attribute, as Ecclesiastes 3:11 indicates.

The Hebrew Language

It is certainly no accident that the Hebrew language is ideal for conveying the type of literature that we find in the Old Testament.

Hebrew is a colorful, somewhat earthy tongue that is marvelously suitable for the narrative portions of the Bible such as Genesis through Esther. It is a story-teller's medium par excellence, and it translates well into all sorts of languages. For example, Hebrew goes into English very nicely indeed—

probably much better than into Latin. (Some may doubt this, but there are no ancient Roman Christians around to contest it!)

The poetic and wisdom literature, Job through Song of Songs, illustrates the poetic potential of Hebrew. Providentially, unlike English poetry, which traditionally depends so heavily on rhyme and meter, Hebrew rhymes its *thoughts* rather than its sounds. By this we mean that much of Hebrew poetry gets its color and light from repeating ideas *in parallel lines* with certain changes for variety. This is called "parallelism." Fortunately, this form can be transmitted into any language without major changes.

The Aramaic Language

If you have ever admired a hand-lettered scroll of the Torah or a nicely printed edition of the Hebrew Bible, the form of these delightfully artistic licorice-black letters that you see is actually borrowed from the Aramaic, a *lingua franca* widely used in the ancient world. It is closely related to Hebrew.

From a biblical viewpoint, this language has several notable features. First and foremost, parts of God's Word, chiefly in Daniel and Ezra, are in this tongue. It has very similar features to Hebrew, but with a bit more flexibility, especially in the use of participles.

A second important fact about this world language is that when the Jews returned from the Babylonian Captivity (sixth century B.C.), many no longer understood Hebrew, so the Bible had to be orally translated into Aramaic in the synagogue readings of the Old Testament. After the Romans drove the Jews out of Palestine (A.D. 138), it was deemed wise to put these oral paraphrases into writing. They were called *Targums*. Sometimes their readings will show up in the footnotes of the NKJV, such as at Genesis 4:15, Psalm 23:6, and Ezekiel 19:10.

Finally, Aramaic is the language in which Mary called Jesus home at suppertime, the language of the earliest church. As such, a few expressions from Aramaic occur in the New Testament.[4]

The Greek Language

Ancient Greek is ideal for communicating truth accurately. The Greeks loved to talk, to discuss, to argue, to philosophize. Their marvelous tongue, spoken in an unbroken stream for over three thousand years, developed precision of verb forms, particles, connectives, and a unique, highly developed usage of the definite article that facilitates the communication of many fine shades of thought.

This aspect of Greek is especially important in doctrinal sections such as Paul's Epistle to the Romans. The flow of thought in that book can be traced from start to finish by means of the little connectives, such as *and, but, then, therefore,* and others. These are retained in the NKJV as in the KJV (see Chapter 11).

Greek is also a beautiful language for literature. While the New Testament has far less of a purely literary approach than the Old, who can long remain blind to the beauties of the Beatitudes, of the Magnificat, of Romans 8, and the Books of Hebrews and James, for example?

In the case of the Old Testament also, the ancient Greek translation of it (still the official translation of the Greek-speaking church) was a vehicle to bring the truths and much of the beauty of the Hebrew Scriptures into a very wide potential readership. For Greek was destined to become the *lingua franca* of the Greco-Roman world, especially in the Eastern part of the Mediterranean basin. This version is called the Septuagint.

Splendors of the Septuagint

"Genesis, Exodus, Leviticus, Numbers, Deuteronomy . . ." intones the little Sunday school girl reciting the books of the Old Testament. Without realizing it she is showing our debt to the Greek translation of the Old Testament. Called the "Septuagint" from the Latin word for *seventy,* this book was a milestone in translation history from any perspective. The very *names* of many of the books are from the Greek translation rather than from the original Hebrew.[5] *Genesis* is Greek for *beginning, Exodus* for the *way out, Deuteronomy* means *second law,* and *Numbers* is the English translation of *Arithmoi,* the Septuagint's title for the fourth Book of Moses.

What is the origin of this first major translation of the Old Testament into a world language? It was produced to fill a deeply felt need of the Jewish community in Alexandria of Egypt in the third and second centuries B.C. Hebrew was becoming less and less known by the majority of Jews, especially young people. What else could they have done to keep from slipping into total biblical ignorance and finally assimilation into the pagan Gentile world around them?

The traditions surrounding the Septuagint (abbreviated LXX) are more colorful than credible. The ruler Ptolemy II was said to desire a translation of the Sacred Scriptures of the Jews for the famous library in Alexandria. According to one account, seventy Hebrew scholars came down to Egypt to put the Pentateuch into Greek (hence the name of the version). Tradition has it that each scholar retired to his private chamber to do the work. When all were finished, the different Greek manuscripts were said to be all identical—to a word!

The Pentateuch was carefully done, and the rest of the books with varying degrees of success. It is well worth noting that this first great step in the Bible for the world was generally a conservative, "formal-equivalence" (or "complete-equivalence," see Chapter 11) type of translation.

Our Latin Legacy

"Latin is a dead language,
As dead as dead can be,
First it killed the Romans,
And now it's killing me!"

This somewhat less than classical quatrain remains in my mind from the high school Latin play. It got a good laugh in the 1950s. The gist of the play, however, was that Latin is alive and well in Washington, D.C., among other places. Latin is also alive and well in a modified form in the English language. Fully sixty-five percent of our tongue is derived from Latin, either directly through early Christian missionaries to England, and later through scholarship, or indirectly through the Norman French invasion.[6]

Since Latin is a complex and highly inflected language (many endings to memorize!), we can't expect English, which has dropped the similar complex structure of the Anglo-Saxon or Old English era, to keep much of the grammar and word order of the Latin Bible. And it doesn't.

Though Greek was the common (*koinē*) tongue of ancient Rome even in the Imperial City (Paul's Letter to the church at Rome was in Greek, not Latin), a need soon grew up for God's Word in Latin. Such early products were called the Old Latin.

However, since so many people knew *some* Greek, nearly everyone seemed to be making a Latin translation of the New Testament. Things became so confusing that Damasus, Bishop of Rome from 366 to 384, commissioned the scholar Hieronymus (St. Jerome) to make a *standard* version of God's Word in Latin. This Bible, called the Vulgate, after fierce initial opposition (all Bibles receive opposition!) became the standard for Western Christendom for a whole millennium. Not a bad fulfillment of Jerome's commission!

The King James translators were all Latin scholars. The notes of their meetings were kept, not in English, but in Latin! We are not surprised, then, that much Christian theological vocabulary is derived from the Latin, enshrined in the KJV and passed on to readers in the NKJV and some other Bibles.

Even someone who doesn't read Latin is able to see something recognizable in the nouns we have italicized in 1 Corinthians 1:31: "Ex ipso autem vos estis in Christo Jesu, qui factus est sapientia nobis a Dei, et *justitia,* et *sanctificatio,* et *redemptio* . . ."

To those words we could add *crux* (cross), *gloria, gratia* (grace), *praedestinatio, propitiatio, reconciliatio, resurrectio, Scriptura, spiritus,* and many more.

Truly, even our basically Germanic English Bible is rich in lovely Latin roots.

So these are some of the various stocks—Hebrew, Aramaic, Greek, and Latin—that have been hybridized to produce the exquisite flowering that eventually produced the majestic Tyndale—King James tradition.

NOTES

[1]The incomparable state flower of Texas!

[2]C. S. Lewis, "The Literary Impact of the Authorized Version." In *Selected Literary Essays,* edited by Walter Hooper.

[3]Milton C. Fisher, "The Pattern of Sound Words: An Essential Quality in Bible Translation," unpublished review of the New King James Version.

[4]Examples include *abba, maranatha,* and *talitha, cumi.*

[5]The Jewish method of referring to the books of the Pentateuch is by their first few words in Hebrew.

[6]For a fascinating account of the French, Latin, and other influences on English, see Robert Claiborne, *Our Marvelous Native Tongue,* especially chapters 5 and 6. Chapter 7, "The Verie Height," is about Shakespeare and the King James Bible.

6

Something New

Solomon was right when he wrote that there was "nothing new under the sun"—at least in the absolute sense. Newness, as we know it, actually consists of a fresh approach, a unique arrangement, a different perception of previous thoughts and facts that are brought forward to our present view. The New King James Version is "new" in this sense. Certainly our chapters, "A Firm Foundation," "A Royal Legacy," and "Something Old," show how very indebted we are to the past, in particular to God's continued grace through the ages in revealing and preserving His Word.

However, we don't wish merely to revel in past tradition. We want to build afresh on the labors of our predecessors, expanding and improving our standard version of the Bible for the present and the future. We feel this to be a more profitable and solid procedure than beginning *totally* anew with each generation, thus falling into the pitfalls that all such experiments are prone to. We ought not to impoverish ourselves by refusing to draw from the labors, successes, and failures of those who have gone before. As a noted journalist has observed, "The past is not dead. It isn't even *past.*"

Just as Chapters 2 and 3 emphasize new details that improve the *accuracy* of the NKJV over past editions of the KJV tradition, so the present chapter describes some of the features that we believe improve the *beauty* of our English Bible.

Styling

The earliest (1611) edition of the King James Bible is extremely difficult for modern readers to understand, as illustrated by the samples shown previously in Chapter 1, "A Firm Foundation." Even the popular 1769 edition, the King James Version commonly used since that date, is discouraging reading for most new users today. Not only the spelling and punctuation, but also the order of words and phrases in sentences, are often confusing.

Therefore, while the true sense of a New King James passage was being established at different levels of review, the process of re-styling for clarity was being performed simultaneously as a separate discipline. Painstaking care was equally exercised in this process to maintain the lyrical grandeur that has popularized the King James Bible throughout its illustrious history—always keeping in view the primary concern for precision of translation.

As warranted, poetic and prose sections are clarified in the NKJV by adding quotation marks, substituting semicolons for KJV colons, using colons to introduce phrases and clauses, and dividing long sentences where expedient. Sometimes, however, the power of a passage is unfolded by the cascading sequence of clauses in a long sentence, as in Ephesians 1:1-6.

In combination with other contemporary modifications in English style, including careful shifts in word order, minor features of re-punctuation eliminate much of the reader's difficulty with former editions of the King James Bible. Precise understanding of the thought is thus enhanced.

Poetry with a Purpose

Since so much of the Old Testament is poetry, it would be difficult for the reader of the New King James Version not to notice the new poetic format that greatly improves readability. If you leaf through *The Oxford Book of English Verse, The Oxford Book of American Verse,* or *The Christian Book of Mystical Verse,* to take just three deservedly popular books of poetry, you will notice that most poems in English have the left margin "justified," or lined up straight, and the right margins ending wherever the line does. Also, these lines, even when not beginning a new sentence, are generally *capitalized.*

Because the KJV has always printed poetry in the same style as it did prose, many readers have been unaware how much poetry there actually is in the Bible. At least three avid KJV readers have told the author: "I hate poetry!" Judging by the Old Testament Psalms, Proverbs, and the Prophets, apparently the Lord does not!

In 1885 a first attempt was made to indicate poetry by special indentation in the English Revised Version. The American Standard Version of 1901 and its updated editions, the Revised Standard Version of 1952, and the New American Standard Bible[1] of 1971, continued this policy.

The NKJV is thus by no means unique in presenting poetic sections as poetry. However, the format is a decided improvement over the older revisions and certainly a great deal more attractive than the KJV's failure to distinguish poetry from prose at all.

Compare, for example, the famous poem on "time" in Ecclesiastes 3:1-8 in the old format and the new:

KJV	NKJV

KJV

1 To every thing there is a season, and a time to every purpose under the heaven:
2 A time to be born, and a time to die; a time to plant, and a time to pluck up that which is planted;
3 A time to kill, and a time to heal; a time to break down, and a time to build up;
4 A time to weep, and a time to laugh; a time to mourn, and a time to dance;
5 A time to cast away stones, and a time to gather stones together; a time to embrace, and a time to refrain from embracing;
6 A time to get, and a time to lose; a time to keep, and a time to cast away;
7 A time to rend, and a time to sew; a time to keep silence, and a time to speak;
8 A time to love, and a time to hate; a time of war, and a time of peace.

NKJV

1 To everything there is a season,
A time for every purpose under
heaven:
2 A time to be born,
And a time to die;
A time to plant,
And a time to pluck what is
planted;
3 A time to kill,
And a time to heal;
A time to break down,
And a time to build up;
4 A time to weep,
And a time to laugh;
A time to mourn,
And a time to dance;
5 A time to cast away stones,
And a time to gather stones;
A time to embrace,
And a time to refrain from
embracing;
6 A time to gain,
And a time to lose;
A time to keep,
And a time to throw away;
7 A time to tear,
And a time to sew;
A time to keep silence,
And a time to speak;
8 A time to love,
And a time to hate;
A time of war,
And a time of peace.

The very structure of the thought is enhanced by the NKJV's presentation of the words on the page.

Another nice thing about printing poetry as poetry is that one can leaf through such a historical book as Genesis, for example, and quickly note ancient Hebrew verse appearing here and there throughout the sacred text. As early as Genesis 2:23 we see Adam's poetic description of his newly acquired wife, and as late as chapter 49 we have Jacob's long prophetic poem about the future of his twelve sons.

God is a Poet! We, too, should learn to appreciate poetry.

Special Formats

The Old Testament in the New

Unique to the NKJV, as recently observed, is the method of indicating Old Testament quotations in the New. It is very helpful for Bible students to know what in the New Testament is a direct citation from the Old. Some have used *italics* to indicate them, but the KJV/NKJV tradition italicizes *supplied* words to smooth out the English translation. Other methods are **bold face** or ALL CAPITALS. We found these methods to be unaesthetic and tending to give too much emphasis to Old Testament quotations.

Our solution was to use a typeface called "oblique." It looks somewhat like italics but can be distinguished if examined carefully. For example, note the following quotation in Hebrews 5:6:

KJV	NKJV
6 As he saith also in another *place,* Thou *art* a priest for ever after the order of Melchisedek.	6 As *He* also *says* in another *place*: *"You* are a *priest forever According to the order of Melchizedek."*

The *He, says,* and *place* are in italics because they are not in the Greek but definitely needed to complete the English. In the quotation itself the only word that is supplied is the understood word *are.* The rest of the quotation is in oblique type. The letters that are obviously different in the two typefaces are the *a's* and *e's,* though there are little differences in all the letters.

New Testament Poetry

Poetic or hymnic writing in the New Testament that is *not* quoted from the Old Testament appears in regular type, such as 1 Timothy 3:16:

KJV	NKJV
16 And without controversy great is the mystery of godliness: God was manifest in the flesh, justified in the Spirit, seen of angels, preached unto the Gentiles, believed on in the world, received up into glory.	16 And without controversy great is the mystery of godliness: God[2] was manifested in the flesh, Justified in the Spirit, Seen by angels, Preached among the Gentiles, Believed on in the world, Received up in glory.

Letters

Another helpful indicator of kind of literature can be seen in correspondence that appears within the body of the text. For example, Nehemiah 6:5-7 quotes Sanballat's unfair and untrue letter as follows:

KJV	NKJV
5 Then sent Sanballath his servant unto me in like manner the fifth time with an open letter in his hand; 6 Wherein was written, It is reported among the heathen, and Gashmu saith it, that thou and the Jews think to rebel: for which cause thou buildest the wall, that thou mayest be their king, according to these words. 7 And thou has also appointed prophets to preach of thee at Jerusalem, saying, There is a king in Judah: and now shall it be reported to the king according to these words. Come now therefore, and let us take counsel together.	5 Then Sanballat sent his servant to me as before, the fifth time, with an open letter in his hand. 6 In it was written: It is reported among the nations, and Geshem says, that you and the Jews plan to rebel; therefore, according to these rumors, you are rebuilding the wall, that you may be their king. 7 And you have also appointed prophets to proclaim concerning you at Jerusalem, saying, "There is a king in Judah!" Now these matters will be reported to the king. So come, therefore, and let us consult together.

When entire books are letters, however, such as Romans through Jude, they are not put in this indented form. The three components of ancient letters—the writer, the addressee, and the greeting—are helpfully indicated, as in 1 Thessalonians 1:1 by the spacing between the three elements:

KJV	NKJV
PAUL, and Silvanus, and Timotheus, unto the church of the Thessalonians which is in God the Father and in the Lord Jesus Christ: Grace be unto you, and peace, from God our Father, and the Lord Jesus Christ.	PAUL, Silvanus, and Timothy, To the church of the Thessalonians in God the Father and the Lord Jesus Christ: Grace to you and peace from God our Father and the Lord Jesus Christ.

The Ten Commandments

The NKJV uses another special format for the Ten Commandments (Ex. 20:1-17), thus making the separate commands stand out clearly:

KJV	NKJV
AND God spake all these words, saying, 2 I am the LORD thy God, which have brought thee out of the land of Egypt, out of the house of bondage. 3 Thou shalt have no other gods before me. 4 Thou shalt not make unto thee any graven image, or any likeness of any thing that is in heaven above, or that is in the earth beneath, or that is in the water under the earth: 5 Thou shalt not bow down thyself to them, nor serve them: for I the LORD thy God am a jealous God, visiting the iniquity of the fathers upon the children unto the third and fourth generations of them that hate me; 6 And shewing mercy unto thousands of them that love me, and keep my commandments.	And God spoke all these words, saying: 2 "I am the LORD your God, who brought you out of the land of Egypt, out of the house of bondage. 3 "You shall have no other gods before Me. 4 "You shall not make for yourself a carved image—any likeness of anything that is in heaven above, or that is in the earth beneath, or that is in the water under the earth; 5 you shall not bow down to them nor serve them. For I, the LORD your God, am a jealous God, visiting the iniquity of the fathers upon the children to the third and fourth generations of those who hate Me, 6 but showing mercy to thousands, to those who love Me and keep My commandments.

7 Thou shalt not take the name of the LORD thy God in vain; for the LORD will not hold him guiltless that taketh his name in vain.
8 Remember the sabbath day, to keep it holy.
9 Six days shalt thou labour, and do all thy work:
10 But the seventh day is the sabbath of the LORD thy God: in it thou shalt not do any work, thou, nor thy son, nor thy daughter, thy manservant, nor thy maidservant, nor thy cattle, nor thy stranger that is within thy gates:
11 For in six days the LORD made heaven and earth, the sea, and all that in them is, and rested the seventh day: wherefore the LORD blessed the sabbath day, and hallowed it.
12 Honour thy father and thy mother: that thy days may be long upon the land which the LORD thy God giveth thee.
13 Thou shalt not kill.
14 Thou shalt not commit adultery.
15 Thou shalt not steal.
16 Thou shalt not bear false witness against thy neighbour.
17 Thou shalt not covet thy neighbour's house, thou shalt not covet thy neighbour's wife, nor his manservant, nor his maidservant, nor his ox, nor his ass, nor any thing that is thy neighbour's.

7 "You shall not take the name of the LORD your God in vain, for the LORD will not hold him guiltless who takes His name in vain.
8 "Remember the Sabbath day, to keep it holy.
9 Six days you shall labor and do all your work,
10 but the seventh day is the Sabbath of the LORD your God. In it you shall do no work: you, nor your son, nor your daughter, nor your male servant, nor your female servant, nor your cattle, nor your stranger who is within your gates.
11 For in six days the LORD made the heavens and the earth, the sea, and all that is in them, and rested the seventh day. Therefore the LORD blessed the Sabbath day and hallowed it.
12 "Honor your father and your mother, that your days may be long upon the land which the LORD your God is giving you.
13 "You shall not murder.
14 "You shall not commit adultery.
15 "You shall not steal.
16 "You shall not bear false witness against your neighbor.
17 "You shall not covet your neighbor's house; you shall not covet your neighbor's wife, nor his male servant, nor his female servant, nor his ox, nor his donkey, nor anything that is your neighbor's.

None of these innovations is for the sake of mere novelty. Rather, our desire is to make the NKJV a most attractive and readable version of God's Word—a work of beauty and a joy to read.

NOTES

[1]See first note in the Introduction.

[2]The reading *God (Theos)* is in ninety-seven percent of the Greek manuscripts. The rest are divided between "who" (*hos*) and "which" (*ho*). See Chapter 10 for more information on New Testament textual data.

7

Something Borrowed

The talented Irish dramatist George Bernard Shaw was no friend to the religion of the Bible. In fact he was an avowed humanist. Nevertheless, as a successful author he felt compelled to admire the talents of the "learned men" of 1611 (as they are rightly called) who produced the Authorized Version. Shaw wrote:

> The translation was extraordinarily well done because to the translators what they were translating was not merely a curious collection of ancient books written by different authors in different stages of culture, but the Word of God divinely revealed through His chosen and expressly inspired scribes. In this conviction they carried out their work with boundless reverence and care and *achieved a beautifully artistic result* (emphasis added).[1]

It is because of what even one who was unfriendly to the faith called "a beautifully artistic result" that we have left so many lovely passages in the KJV largely intact, merely updating the archaic and occasionally even obsolete vocabulary, syntax, and punctuation.

Of the many such passages to choose from, we here present eight of the most beloved of all, four from each Testament:

Old Testament Selections

The Creation — Genesis 1:1-13

KJV	NKJV
IN the beginning God created the heaven and the earth.	IN the beginning God created the heavens and the earth.
2 And the earth was without form, and void; and darkness was upon the face of the deep. And the Spirit of God moved upon the face of the waters.	2 The earth was without form, and void; and darkness was on the face of the deep. And the Spirit of God was hovering over the face of the waters.

71

3 And God said, Let there be light: and there was light.
4 And God saw the light, that it was good: and God divided the light from the darkness.
5 And God called the light Day, and the darkness he called Night. And the evening and the morning were the first day.
6 And God said, Let there be a firmament in the midst of the waters, and let it divide the waters from the waters.
7 And God made the firmament, and divided the waters which were under the firmament from the waters which were above the firmament: and it was so.
8 And God called the firmament Heaven. And the evening and the morning were the second day.
9 And God said, Let the waters under the heaven be gathered together unto one place, and let the dry land appear: and it was so.
10 And God called the dry land Earth; and the gathering together of the waters called he Seas: and God saw that it was good.
11 And God said, Let the earth bring forth grass, the herb yielding seed, and the fruit tree yielding fruit after his kind, whose seed is in itself, upon the earth: and it was so.
12 And the earth brought forth grass, and herb yielding seed after his kind, and the tree yielding fruit, whose seed was in itself, after his kind: and God saw that it was good.
13 And the evening and the morning were the third day.

3 Then God said, "Let there be light"; and there was light.
4 And God saw the light, that it was good; and God divided the light from the darkness.
5 God called the light Day, and the darkness He called Night. So the evening and the morning were the first day.
6 Then God said, "Let there be a firmament in the midst of the waters, and let it divide the waters from the waters."
7 Thus God made the firmament, and divided the waters which were under the firmament from the waters which were above the firmament; and it was so.
8 And God called the firmament Heaven. So the evening and the morning were the second day.
9 Then God said, "Let the waters under the heavens be gathered together into one place, and let the dry land appear"; and it was so.
10 And God called the dry land Earth, and the gathering together of the waters He called Seas. And God saw that it was good.
11 Then God said, "Let the earth bring forth grass, the herb that yields seed, and the fruit tree that yields fruit according to its kind, whose seed is in itself, on the earth"; and it was so.
12 And the earth brought forth grass, the herb that yields seed according to its kind, and the tree that yields fruit, whose seed is in itself according to its kind. And God saw that it was good.
13 So the evening and the morning were the third day.

The Creation narrative is not technically Hebrew poetry, but it borders on being such. Often biblical prose ascends to such rhythmic heights of expression that its effect is very much like the emotional power so characteristic of poetry. Even modern Western prose sometimes achieves this result. The captivating rhythm of repetitive phrases, like "Then God said . . . ," alternating with "And God called . . . ," "And God made . . . ," "And God set . . ." affect us with the grandeur of the events described. Thus it would seem monstrous to bury this rhythm in the prosy journalese of the morning newspaper! And the NKJV refrains from this mistake, as do other sensitive translations of the Scriptures.

The editors thought it valuable to capitalize personal and possessive pronouns of deity throughout the Bible, as with "He" in verse 5. This is a significant reader's aid for clarifying references to deity in all cases.

One is hardly aware of having moved from an earlier to a later edition of the King James Version as he reads this passage in the New King James. And this is exactly the smooth transition, with significant updates of vocabulary, that the translators sought to achieve.

The Shepherd Psalm — Psalm 23

KJV

1 The LORD is my shepherd; I shall not want.
2 He maketh me to lie down in green pastures: he leadeth me beside the still waters.
3 He restoreth my soul: he leadeth me in the paths of righteousness for his name's sake.
4 Yea, though I walk through the valley of the shadow of death, I will fear no evil: for thou art with me; thy rod and thy staff they comfort me.
5 Thou preparest a table before me in the presence of mine enemies: thou anointest my head with oil; my cup runneth over.
6 Surely goodness and mercy shall follow me all the days of my life: and I will dwell in the house of the LORD for ever.

NKJV

1 The LORD is my shepherd;
I shall not want.
2 He makes me to lie down in green pastures;
He leads me beside the still waters.
3 He restores my soul;
He leads me in the paths of righteousness
For His name's sake.
4 Yea, though I walk through the valley of the shadow of death,
I will fear no evil;
For You are with me;
Your rod and Your staff, they comfort me.
5 You prepare a table before me in the presence of my enemies;
You anoint my head with oil;
My cup runs over.
6 Surely goodness and mercy shall follow me
All the days of my life;
And I will dwell in the house of the LORD
Forever.

Voltaire, like Shaw, had an exalted opinion of his own writing style and was no lover of the Bible, yet he called this psalm the *most beautiful thing ever written.* High praise indeed from one who despised traditional religion! Can those to whom it is not only beautiful but also true as well disagree? Most of us know this psalm by heart. Even the *yea* in v. 4 was retained, since the passage is poetry, and *yea* is still understood as an older alternative to the modern *yes.* Verse 6 illustrates a place where the reading of the Masoretic text, *return,* was not used in 1611: *dwell* is from four ancient versions and some Hebrew manuscripts (see NKJV footnotes and Chapter 9). The slight difference in meaning was not thought to be worth the change in such a celebrated psalm. NASB and NIV concur on this.

Rise Up My Love — Song of Songs 2:8-14

KJV	NKJV
8 The voice of my beloved! behold, he cometh leaping upon the mountains, skipping upon the hills.	8 The voice of my beloved! Behold, he comes Leaping upon the mountains, Skipping upon the hills.
9 My beloved is like a roe or a young hart: behold, he standeth behind our wall, he looketh forth at the windows, shewing himself through the lattice.	9 My beloved is like a gazelle or a young stag. Behold, he stands behind our wall; He is looking through the windows, Gazing through the lattice.
10 My beloved spake, and said unto me, Rise up, my love, my fair one, and come away.	10 My beloved spoke, and said to me: "Rise up, my love, my fair one, And come away.
11 For, lo, the winter is past, the rain is over and gone;	11 For lo, the winter is past, The rain is over and gone.
12 The flowers appear on the earth; the time of the singing birds is come, and the voice of the turtle is heard in our land;	12 The flowers appear on the earth; The time of singing has come, And the voice of the turtledove Is heard in our land.
13 The fig tree putteth forth her green figs, and the vines with the tender grape give a good smell. Arise, my love, my fair one, and come away.	13 The fig tree puts forth her green figs, And the vines with the tender grapes Give a good smell. Rise up, my love, my fair one, And come away!

14 O my dove, that art in the clefts of the rock, in the secret places of the stairs, let me see thy countenance, let me hear thy voice; for sweet is thy voice, and thy countenance is comely.

14 "O my dove, in the clefts of the rock,
In the secret places of the cliff,
Let me see your face,
Let me hear your voice;
For your voice is sweet,
And your face is lovely."

The tender invitation from "the beloved" to his Shulamite spouse to "rise up" and follow him into the springtime loveliness of their land will not bear much improvement for sheer beauty. Only a few words of vocabulary required substitution: The "turtle" (verse 12) of course is no longer the name of a bird today ("turtledove"), and "countenance" (verse 14) is rendered better as "face" to sustain cadence with the one-syllable word "voice" at the end of the next line.

The Suffering Savior — Isaiah 53

KJV

1 Who hath believed our report? and to whom is the arm of the LORD revealed?
2 For he shall grow up before him as a tender plant, and as a root out of a dry ground: he hath no form nor comeliness; and when we shall see him, there is no beauty that we should desire him.
3 He is despised and rejected of men; a man of sorrows, and acquainted with grief: and we hid as it were our faces from him; he was despised, and we esteemed him not.
4 Surely he hath borne our griefs, and carried our sorrows: yet we did esteem him stricken, smitten of God, and afflicted.

NKJV

1 Who has believed our report?
And to whom has the arm of
the LORD been revealed?
2 For He shall grow up before
Him as a tender plant,
And as a root out of dry
ground.
He has no form or comeliness;
And when we see Him,
There is no beauty
that we should desire Him.
3 He is despised and rejected
by men,
A Man of sorrows
and acquainted with grief.
And we hid, as it were,
our faces from Him;
He was despised, and we
did not esteem Him.
4 Surely He has borne our griefs
And carried our sorrows;
Yet we esteemed Him stricken,
Smitten by God, and afflicted.

5 But he was wounded for our transgressions, he was bruised for our iniquities: the chastisement of our peace was upon him; and with his stripes we are healed.
6 All we like sheep have gone astray; we have turned every one to his own way; and the LORD hath laid on him the iniquity of us all.
7 He was oppressed, and he was afflicted, yet he opened not his mouth: he is brought as a lamb to the slaughter, and as a sheep before her shearers is dumb, so he openeth not his mouth.
8 He was taken from prison and from judgment: and who shall declare his generation? for he was cut off out of the land of the living: for the transgression of my people was he stricken.
9 And he made his grave with the wicked, and with the rich in his death; because he had done no violence, neither was any deceit in his mouth.
10 Yet it pleased the LORD to bruise him; he hath put him to grief: when thou shalt make his soul an offering for sin, he shall see his seed, he shall prolong his days, and the pleasure of the LORD shall prosper in his hand.
11 He shall see of the travail of his soul, and shall be satisfied: by his knowledge shall my righteous servant justify many; for he shall bear their iniquities.

5 But He was wounded for
    our transgressions,
He was bruised for our iniquities;
The chastisement for our
    peace was upon Him,
And by His stripes we are healed.
6 All we like sheep have gone astray;
We have turned, every one,
    to his own way;
And the LORD has laid on
    Him the iniquity of us all.
7 He was oppressed and He
    was afflicted,
Yet He opened not His mouth;
He was led as a lamb to the
    slaughter,
And as a sheep before its
    shearers is silent,
So He opened not His mouth.
8 He was taken from prison
    and from judgment,
And who will declare His generation?
For He was cut off from the
    land of the living;
For the transgressions of My
    people He was stricken.
9 And they made His grave
    with the wicked—
But with the rich at His death,
Because He had done no violence,
Nor was any deceit in His mouth.
10 Yet it pleased the LORD to bruise
    Him;
He has put Him to grief.
When You make His soul an offering
    for sin,
He shall see His seed,
    He shall prolong His days,
And the pleasure of the LORD
    shall prosper in His hand.
11 He shall see the labor of His
    soul, and be satisfied.
By His knowledge My righteous
    Servant shall justify many,
For He shall bear their iniquities.

12 Therefore will I divide him a portion with the great, and he shall divide the spoil with the strong; because he hath poured out his soul unto death: and he was numbered with the transgressors; and he bare the sin of many, and made intercession for the transgressors.	12 Therefore I will divide Him a portion with the great, And He shall divide the spoil with the strong, Because He poured out His soul unto death, And He was numbered with the transgressors, And He bore the sin of many, And made intercession for the transgressors.

It was passages such as this that made Augustine exclaim that Isaiah was not so much a prophet as an evangelist. Truly one of the most vividly Christ-centered passages in the Old Testament, and rightly treated as such by the apostles of our Lord in the New Testament.

The NKJV changes in Isaiah 53 are minimal, chiefly minor changes in usage since 1769, though some of these help clarify nicely. "The chastisement for [rather than *of*] our peace" makes the *purpose* of Christ's death clearer. In verse 7 the word *dumb* was changed to *silent* because it is popularly used for *stupid* in North America.

The contrast with what the wicked planned for Christ's body—a common grave with criminals—and what wealthy Joseph of Arimathea succeeded in supplying is brought out in verse 9.

The alternative reading of the Dead Sea Scrolls and the Septuagint for verse 11 is interesting but not really superior in context to the Masoretic reading.[2] *Labor* replaces *travail* since the latter is so little used, and *labor* today has the fitting meanings of "hard work" as well as "travailing in birth."

New Testament Selections

The Lord's Prayer — Matthew 6:9-13

KJV

9 After this manner therefore pray ye: Our Father which art in heaven, Hallowed be thy name.
10 Thy kingdom come. Thy will be done in earth, as it is in heaven.

NKJV

9 In this manner, therefore, pray: Our Father in heaven, Hallowed be Your name.
10 Your kingdom come. Your will be done On earth as it is in heaven.

11 Give us this day our daily bread.	11 Give us this day our daily bread.
12 And forgive us our debts, as we forgive our debtors.	12 And forgive us our debts, As we forgive our debtors.
13 And lead us not into temptation, but deliver us from evil: For thine is the kingdom, and the power, and the glory, for ever. Amen.	13 And do not lead us into temptation, But deliver us from the evil one. For Yours is the kingdom and the power and the glory forever. Amen.

Even many of those who use the NKJV in their congregations for preaching, teaching, memory work, and Sunday School still use the older language when saying the Lord's Prayer.

Changing "which art" to "who are" would not be a happy rendering. Since the verb *to be* is not in the original, the correct solution was to translate simply, "Our Father in heaven."

For some people the surprise change is in verse 13. The Greek is ambiguous since the genitive form can be neuter (*evil*) or masculine (*evil one*). There is a separate related abstract noun for evil.[3] Thus the NKJV reading is probably a good one.

As a teenager I asked a brilliant Athenian scientist in our church in Washington D.C. if Greek people praying the Lord's Prayer ever thought of the "evil one" rather than just "evil." Dr. Panai was surprised. Being more versed in the nuances of French than of English, he had assumed we *meant* the "evil one"–Satan—when we said "deliver us from evil." The word *ponēros* is translated "evil one" also in Matthew 5:37, John 17:15, and 2 Thessalonians 3:3.

As to the deletion of the ending of the Lord's Prayer in some versions because it is missing in some ancient manuscripts, we believe this is a mistake. The unfounded theory that early Christians were dissatisfied with the prayer ending on a negative note—either "evil" or "the evil one"–and so "improved" our Lord's model prayer by adapting a passage from Chronicles for liturgical purposes does not commend itself. See the discussion of this matter in Part Three: Completeness.

The Magnificat — Luke 1:46-55

KJV	NKJV
46 And Mary said, My soul doth magnify the Lord,	46 And Mary said: "My soul magnifies the Lord,
47 And my spirit hath rejoiced in God my Saviour.	47 And my spirit has rejoiced in God my Savior.

48 For he hath regarded the low estate of his handmaiden: for, behold, from henceforth all generations shall call me blessed.
49 For he that is mighty hath done to me great things; and holy is his name.
50 And his mercy is on them that fear him from generation to generation.
51 He hath shewed strength with his arm; he hath scattered the proud in the imagination of their hearts.
52 He hath put down the mighty from their seats, and exalted them of low degree.
53 He hath filled the hungry with good things; and the rich he hath sent empty away.
54 He hath holpen his servant Israel, in remembrance of his mercy;
55 As he spake to our fathers, to Abraham, and to his seed for ever.

48 For He has regarded the lowly state of His maidservant;
For behold, henceforth all generations will call me blessed.
49 For He who is mighty has done great things for me,
And holy is His name.
50 And His mercy is on those who fear Him.
From generation to generation.
51 He has shown strength with His arm;
He has scattered the proud in the imagination of their hearts.
52 He has put down the mighty from their thrones,
And exalted the lowly,
53 He has filled the hungry with good things,
And the rich He has sent away empty.
54 He has helped His servant Israel,
In remembrance of His mercy,
55 As He spoke to our fathers,
To Abraham and to his seed forever."

What is most noteworthy about King James prose, as well as its poetry, is the often uncanny combination of simplicity of language with exaltation of thought. The Virgin Mary's song of thanksgiving, traditionally called the Magnificat, may be the chief example of this remarkable fusion of qualities throughout the Bible.

Notice of the few vocabulary improvements is in order: "Low estate" becomes "lowly state," intended to emphasize her humble social status (verse 48); similarly, "them of low degree" becomes simply "lowly" (verse 52); "seats" is now translated "thrones," as the Greek work denotes (verse 52); and "helped" updates "holpen," a very strange word indeed to modern readers (verse 54). Note, however, that "seed" is retained from the older editions of the KJV (verse 55). Here poetic power overrides "descendants," as the original word for "seed" is rendered elsewhere in NKJV prose sections.

The Great Love Chapter — 1 Corinthians 13

KJV	NKJV

1 Though I speak with the tongues of men and of angels, and have not charity, I am become as sounding brass, or a tinkling cymbal.
2 And though I have the gift of prophecy, and understand all mysteries, and all knowledge; and though I have all faith, so that I could remove mountains, and have not charity, I am nothing.
3 And though I bestow all my goods to feed the poor, and though I give my body to be burned, and have not charity, it profiteth me nothing.
4 Charity suffereth long, and is kind; charity envieth not; charity vaunteth not itself, is not puffed up.
5 Doth not behave itself unseemly, seeketh not her own, is not easily provoked, thinketh no evil;
6 Rejoiceth not in iniquity, but rejoiceth in the truth.
7 Beareth all things, believeth all things, hopeth all things, endureth all things.
8 Charity never faileth: but whether there be prophecies, they shall fail; whether there be tongues, they shall cease; whether there be knowledge, it shall vanish away.
9 For we know in part, and we prophesy in part.
10 But when that which is perfect is come, then that which is in part shall be done away.
11 When I was a child, I spake as a child, I understood as a child, I thought as a child: but when I became a man, I put away childish things.
12 For now we see through a glass, darkly; but then face to face: now I know in part; but then shall I know even as also I am known.

1 Though I speak with the tongues of men and of angels, but have not love, I have become sounding brass or a clanging cymbal.
2 And though I have the gift of prophecy, and understand all mysteries and all knowledge, and though I have all faith, so that I could remove mountains, but have not love, I am nothing.
3 And though I bestow all my goods to feed the poor, and though I give my body to be burned, but have not love, it profits me nothing.
4 Love suffers long and is kind; love does not envy; love does not parade itself, is not puffed up;
5 does not behave rudely, does not seek its own, is not provoked, thinks no evil;
6 does not rejoice in iniquity, but rejoices in the truth;
7 bears all things, believes all things, hopes all things, endures all things.
8 Love never fails. But whether there are prophecies, they will fail; whether there are tongues, they will cease; whether there is knowledge, it will vanish away.
9 For we know in part and we prophesy in part.
10 But when that which is perfect has come, then that which is in part will be done away.
11 When I was a child, I spoke as a child, I understood as a child, I thought as a child; but when I became a man, I put away childish things.
12 For now we see in a mirror dimly, but then face to face. Now I know in part, but then shall I know just as I also am known.

13 And now abideth faith, hope, charity, these three; but the greatest of these is charity.	13 And now abide faith, hope, love, these three; but the greatest of these is love.

Most readers of the KJV learn sooner or later that *charity* in this passage in 1611 did not mean what it does today. The KJV scholars chose *charity* partly under the influence of the Latin Vulgate, which has *charitas* here. They wanted a word without the carnal connotations that we now associate with the spelling "luv." All modern versions part company with the KJV here, since giving to "charities" is only a small subdivision of Christian *agapē*, the well-known Greek word.

The change from *tinkling* to *clanging* is necessary since the former word now suggests a delicate, frosty sound, quite unlike a cymbal. The archaic "vaunteth not itself" is vividly updated to "love does not parade itself."

In verse 5 "puffed up" is good poetry and still communicates pride very well. The word *rudely* is much more appropriate than *unseemly* today. *Easily* is deleted simply because it is not in any reading of the original text! Were the translators of 1611 attempting to make it "easier" for us by inserting it? We don't know.

The interpretation of verse 10 is very much debated, so it is important to retain the literal translation. Let the reader, student, preacher, or teacher tell us what it *means* and let the text be what it *says*.

The *glass* in verse 12 is short for "looking glass," but millions don't know this. Actually the word is not quite accurate, since ancient mirrors were not glass but highly polished metal. The KJV *glass* was a seventeenth century "dynamic-equivalence" translation[4] (like *candle* for *lamp,* and quite valid for 1611).

Dimly (KJV *darkly*) in verse 12 represents literally "in an enigma" (*en ainigmati*), but this expression is too obscure for most readers. A very refined reporter for the *Manchester Guardian* regretted the NKJV's loss of "through a glass darkly," indeed a great phrase. However, this is a place where communicating *truth* must overshadow literary *beauty.* The NKJV may not be quite as artistic in this phrase, but it is a much clearer mirror of Paul's thought.

Worthy Is the Lamb — *Revelation 5:9-13*

KJV	NKJV

KJV

9 And they sung a new song, saying, Thou art worthy to take the book, and to open the seals thereof: for thou wast slain, and hast redeemed us to God by thy blood out of every kindred, and tongue, and people, and nation;
10 And hast made us unto our God kings and priests: and we shall reign on the earth.
11 And I beheld, and I heard the voice of many angels round about the throne and the beasts and the elders: and the number of them was ten thousand times ten thousand, and thousands of thousands;
12 Saying with a loud voice, Worthy is the Lamb that was slain to receive power, and riches, and wisdom, and strength, and honour, and glory, and blessing.
13 And every creature which is in heaven, and on the earth, and under the earth, and such as are in the sea, and all that are in them, heard I saying, Blessing, and honour, and glory, and power, be unto him that sitteth upon the throne, and unto the Lamb for ever and ever.

NKJV

9 And they sang a new song, saying:

"You are worthy to take the scroll,
And to open its seals;
For You were slain,
And have redeemed us to God by
  Your blood
Out of every tribe and tongue
  and people and nation,
10 And have made us kings and priests
  to our God;
And we shall reign on the
  earth."

11 Then I looked, and I heard the voice of many angels around the throne, the living creatures, and the elders; and the number of them was ten thousand times ten thousand, and thousands of thousands,
12 saying with a loud voice:

"Worthy is the Lamb who was slain
To receive power and riches
  and wisdom,
And strength and honor and glory
  and blessing!"

13 And every creature which is in heaven and on the earth and under the earth and such as are in the sea, and all that are in them, I heard saying:

"Blessing and honor and glory
  and power
Be to Him who sits on the throne,
And to the Lamb, forever and ever!"

Perhaps the most elevating songs of the Bible are found in the triumphant Book of Revelation. In John's throne-room vision, for example, we see Christ the Lamb about to receive the scroll (technically more accurate than KJV's "book") delivered from the hand of the Father. Just at this moment the twenty-four elders fall down before the Lamb and sing the incomparable lines of verses 9 and 10.

Following this song, the elders are joined by myriads of heavenly singers, along with every creature of creation, in the glad anthem, "Worthy is the Lamb," that Handel set to such magnificent music.

Except for the necessary corrections of archaic vocabulary and grammar, the basic structure of this New Testament psalm is unchanged in the NKJV. The earlier translation's beauty has been retouched only in that the lyrics have properly been recast as poetic lines.

If we had a much larger volume we could multiply examples of borrowed beauty in the NKJV, but these eight passages should suffice to demonstrate how carefully we have retained the noble phrasing of the Tyndale—King James tradition, all the while bringing the version into the soon-emerging turn of the century.

NOTES

[1]Introduction to *The Holy Bible, The New King James Version* (first edition 1982), p. iii.

[2]They read "from the labor of His soul He shall see light." (See NKJV note.) The NIV builds its interpretation on this variant reading.

[3]The Greek *tou ponērou* here can be the genitive of *ho ponēros* ("the evil one") or of *to ponēron* ("evil"). The unambiguous form for evil in the abstract would be the genitive of *hē ponēria,* a feminine noun.

[4]See Chapter 11, "Complete Equivalence in Translation" for this term.

8

Something Blue

It happened not many years ago. A Christian businessman was bringing a new believer to a Gideon's "encampment." Part of the proceedings included reading a Bible passage around in a circle, each man reading a verse. This posed a problem for the new believer who was not a good reader, and besides, the text was the King James Version. The businessman was afraid the young man might be humiliated if he stumbled in reading his verse.

As the men took their places in the circle, our businessman was horrified to read ahead and observe that his friend would be reading a verse with a word in it that is nowadays considered vulgar! It was one of those passages in the Books of the Kings that uses a rather earthy Hebrew idiom for a male.[1]

When the new Christian's turn came, he read out in a loud, clear voice, ". . . he slew all the house of Baasha: he left him not one that *pissayeth* against a wall . . ." (1 Kings 16:11). The Old English verb ending plus the accidental addition of an extra syllable saved the day. The reader was totally unaware of what he had read, and the good Gideon breathed a sigh of relief!

A Matter of Good Taste

This true story is told, not to amuse, but to illustrate the fact that the 1769 text still retains a number of readings that were once quite acceptable in polite society, but which cause embarrassment in church circles today. The contemporary mass media often revel in vulgar language. But is it right for Christian children to find in their Bibles what they are taught are "no-no" words elsewhere? We think not. The Hebrew idiom "he that pisseth against a wall" means literally no more and no less than "a male." Therefore NKJV, e.g., reads simply ". . . he killed all the household of Baasha; he did not leave him one *male* . . . ." The passages mentioned have absolutely nothing to do with necessary bodily functions as such.

The noun form of this questionable verb occurs in 2 Kings 18:27 and its parallel text in Isaiah 36:12: ". . . hath he not sent me to the men that sit upon the wall, that they may eat their own *dung,* and drink their own *piss* with you?"

This was an unpleasant remark, but the enemy wanted to communicate the terrible state of affairs that a military siege would produce. The NKJV communicates the *facts* without the 1611 *words* that are no longer in good taste: ". . . to the men who sit on the wall, who will *eat* and *drink* their own *waste* with you" (Isaiah 36:12).

The word *dung* is still acceptable in some contexts, but certainly is not needed today as much as the KJV uses it. For example, compare the two New Testament occurrences of this word with their modernization in NKJV:

"Lord,[2] let it alone this year also, till I shall dig about it, and dung it" (Luke 13:8, KJV).

"Sir,[2] let it alone this year also, until I dig around it and fertilize it" (Luke 13:8, NKJV).

Philippians 3:8, a famous verse, likewise can be improved upon:

Yea doubtless, and I count all things but loss for the excellency of the knowledge of Christ Jesus my Lord: for whom I have suffered the loss of all things, and do count them but dung, that I may win Christ (KJV).

Yet indeed I also count all things loss for the excellence of the knowledge of Christ Jesus my Lord, for whom I have suffered the loss of all things, and count them as rubbish, that I may gain Christ (NKJV).

Now if the Greek word *definitely* meant waste products, *dung* would have been left here in the NKJV. But it does not! The Greek word *skybala* is thought by some to be from an expression "throw to the dogs"—hence *garbage* or *rubbish*. Another view is that it comes from *skōr,* an expression meaning *dung*.[3] Since we are not sure, *rubbish* is a good choice.

Catalogs of Vice

Another word family that disturbs many people is the "wh— words": *whore, whorish, whoredom, whoring,* and *whoremonger.* These are borderline words. They are not nasty, but they often shock people of cultivated taste. The KJV translates the Hebrew and Greek words for *whore* very often by the similar but more acceptable term, *harlot.* Since this word was already part of the King James tradition, the NKJV uses it in all places where *whore* occurred. The Executive Review Committees of both the Old and New Testaments considered using the word *prostitute,* but rejected it as being on a lower literary level than the KJV word *harlot.*

Five times in the New Testament the word *whoremonger* occurs, each time in lists[4] of gross sins. The Greek word is *pornos,*[5] which is also translated *fornicator* five times in the KJV. Where this term is used in a *general* sense in the NKJV, it is translated *sexually immoral.* Where it occurs next to other *specific* sexual sins, like adultery or homosexuality, the more precise English word for illicit sex between unmarried people—*fornication*—is used. The NKJV uses *fornicator(s)* six times and the abstract noun *fornication(s)* sixteen times, all but once in New Testament texts.

Because sexual sin is rampant in modern society, it seems relevant to retain the biblical terms rather than to conform to softened secular usages. "Premarital sex," "extramarital sex," and "gay sex" are morally anemic substitutes for plain "fornication," "adultery," and "sodomy."

We have discussed some words that are rather unpleasant to many people of decent sensibilities, and to Christians in particular. But they are facts of life on this planet. Nevertheless, we can translate the terms so as to communicate the truth without violating the canons of good taste.

We have no desire to pillory the seventeenth-century translators. What was good and acceptable English then may not be so today. Hence the need for periodic updates of the Bible to correct contemporary usage.

The excision of needlessly offensive language from the King James tradition can only improve the text.[6] In this respect most people will probably agree that the beauty of the NKJV is enhanced.

The Affections

Modern hospitals generally refer to elimination of waste by certain euphemisms, like "B.M." There is nothing wrong with the old word *bowel,* when used literally, but many people are uncomfortable with the word and are reluctant to use it in public.

Seventeenth century society had no such qualms. The King James Bible used *bowels* thirty-one times in the Old Testament, translating three Hebrew terms. The King James New Testament, translating just one Greek word, used *bowels* nine times.

Interestingly enough, the word in the Bible seldom refers to the literal intestines, but usually is figurative for the emotions or affections.

The NKJV totally updates this old word in all forty places, choosing words that best fit the context.

Perhaps the most unfortunate occurrence of the old word is in Song of Songs 5:4. The context is one of love and beauty—until (in the KJV) the Shulamite says of her beloved, "and my *bowels were moved* for him." Not only does this phrase spoil the loveliness of the passage today, but it definitely does not mean what modern usage might imply. The NKJV update, "my heart yearned for him," communicates exactly what the clause means.

In Greek the word *splangchna* is used once literally. When Judas' body fell from the rope after he hanged himself, "all his *entrails* gushed out" (Acts 1:18)—not an attractive scene, but an accurate portrayal!

Eight times this term is used in a figurative sense of the affections in the New Testament, for example 2 Corinthians 6:12; Philippians 1:8; 2:1.

In at least two cases the King James rendering is embarrassing to read in a church service. The following King James and New King James renderings illustrate this:

"For God is my record, how greatly I long after you all in the <u>bowels</u> of Jesus Christ" Philippians 1:8, (KJV).	"For God is my witness, how greatly I long for you all with the <u>affection</u> of Jesus Christ" Philippians 1:8, (NKJV).
"Yea, brother, let me have joy of thee in the Lord: refresh my <u>bowels</u> in the Lord" Philemon 20, (KJV).	"Yes, brother, let me have joy from you in the Lord; refresh my <u>heart</u> in the Lord" Philemon 20, (NKJV).

On the one hand many modern writers commonly ridicule euphemisms and prefer to express things bluntly, crudely, or with intent to shock the reader. We may be criticized for being prudish by such writers. Yet the Bible itself uses euphemisms. For example, Genesis 4:1 says that "Adam *knew* (Hebrew *yāda'*) his wife Eve." The result was conception and childbirth. The NIV translates this "Adam lay with his wife Eve." The NKJV kept the literal rendering for two reasons. First it seems in better taste. If Moses felt a restrained expression was superior, and all who need to know will know what it means, why change it? Secondly, the Hebrew verb has deeper and richer meaning than the merely physical. It is the same word used of God's intimate knowledge of His people Israel (Amos 3:2).

There are other euphemisms in Hebrew, such as the expression "to cover one's feet." This idiom, translated literally in the older King James (1 Samuel 24:3), is so unclear in English that many think it means that Saul lay down in the cave and put a robe over his feet. Actually, he was performing a bodily function of elimination, for which there are several modern English idioms.

Thus, one of the guidelines for the NKJV translators and editors was to correct all words and expressions that, while quite acceptable in earlier English, are now considered vulgar. We believe that most people will agree that these words are by no means a necessary part of the actual meaning of the sacred text. But they enhance the beauty of the NKJV—*by not being there!*

NOTES

[1] There are four such expressions in 1 and 2 Kings, and two in 1 Samuel 25:22, 34.

[2] The same Greek word (*kyrios*) can mean "Lord" or "Sir." In the 1611 edition it probably means the "lord" of the vineyard in the parable itself.

[3] A. T. Robertson, *Word Pictures in the New Testament,* Vol. V, p. 453.

[4] The technical term for such lists is "vice catalogs."

[5] Our word *pornography* ("harlot-writing) comes from this same Greek root word.

[6] The older words for *donkey* and *rooster,* for example, generally bring needless snickers from schoolboys in Sunday school.

PART THREE:
COMPLETENESS

"Become complete" (2 Corinthians 13:11a).

In Parts One and Two, we have highlighted the accuracy and beauty of the NKJV. Now we turn to a third distinctive of the NKJV: Completeness. Since *complete* is a very inclusive word, we should explain what we mean by the term. In this section, "complete" does not mean "exhaustive." Instead, it means full, inclusive, not lacking in any essential element.

In French a man's suit is called *un complet*, not that it includes shirt and tie, but that it is a full suit of clothes. Likewise, *The Complete Concordance to the Bible, New King James Version*, is "complete" in that it gives a full account of the words chosen. It does not give an exhaustive list of such words as *and, but, from, with,* or other very common words that most people would never choose in looking up a verse in a concordance.

With this general definition in mind, the NKJV demonstrates its completeness in the following ways:

9. Complete Old Testament Textual Data. This chapter not only tells about the Hebrew and Aramaic texts, but also a little about the variant readings from the ancient versions and the Dead Sea Scrolls.

10. Complete New Testament Textual Data. Chapter 9 shows how every page of the NKJV New Testament presents, not just one textual viewpoint (as most modern Bibles do), but three: the traditional, the critical, and the majority text views.

11. Complete Equivalence in Translation. This is the interesting account of how a careful and conservative translation can communicate a relatively complete rendering in both meaning and form, aided as well by dynamic-equivalent renderings where needed for good idiomatic English.

Conclusion. The final chapter summarizes the three emphases of the book—Accuracy, Beauty, and Completeness, illustrated with quotations from many sources.

9

Complete Old Testament Textual Data

The ancient Jewish scholars who preserved the Hebrew Old Testament Scriptures—the Torah, the Prophets, and the Writings, as they would call them[1]—are to be congratulated for the meticulous care with which they copied the Word of God by hand.

When we consider the span of time it took to write the original manuscripts of the Hebrew Scriptures (about a millennium),[2] the length of these Scriptures (three times longer than the New Testament), and the fact that the text was hand-copied without vowels in ancient times, their work was stupendous! Then add to these hurdles the periodic persecutions of Jews by Gentile neighbors or foreign invaders, such as the notorious Antiochus Epiphanes (who sought to utterly destroy the Jewish faith), and the generally excellent state of the Hebrew text is almost miraculous. The *copies* were not made by divine inspiration, so there was no true miracle in copying the Scriptures. But there is evidence of a high degree of providential care, since there are such a small number of copyist's errors. God gave to Jews and Christians the task of preserving His originally inspired words.

The Ancient Scrolls

As the various Old Testament authors penned their inspired books, the nation of Israel added these writings to the sacred volume, beginning with the Torah, or the five Books of Moses. These books are popularly referred to as "the Pentateuch" (Greek for "five-sheath"), so-called from the way the scrolls in ancient libraries were stored in receptacles somewhat like sword sheaths.

Many people erroneously think that the Old Testament is merely the "literature" of the Hebrew people. In reality, there were many other Jewish books during and after the completion of the Hebrew canon, the official collection of authoritative and divinely inspired works. For example, the

Old Testament mentions several historical works, such as "the Book of Jasher" (Joshua 10:13; 2 Samuel 1:18), that are not part of the Scriptures. Between the writing of the Old and New Testaments (and after) many interesting Jewish religious works were written. Those called "Apocrypha" (Greek for "hidden") were never accepted as inspired by the Jews. Some were not even written in Hebrew or Aramaic. These books were also rejected as noncanonical by the Protestants, though they are considered as a secondary canon ("deuterocanonical") by the Greek Orthodox and the Roman Catholics.

While these books contain much valuable historical, linguistic, and religious material, they also contain many contradictions to the canonical books. Also, the moral and spiritual tone is often sub-biblical.

The Masoretic Text

Unlike the situation in the New Testament, where there are a number of differing theories as to the best manuscripts to emphasize in constructing a printed Greek text, most Old Testament scholars lean very heavily on the traditional Masoretic Text. This text is so-called from "Masoretes," a name for textual scholars which was derived from the Hebrew word for *tradition.* Before the Masoretes the Hebrew Bible had been passed down from generation to generation by ancient scribes who scrupulously copied the original text. By the sixth century A.D. their work had been taken over by the Masoretes who continued to preserve the sacred text in a form known as the Masoretic Text. The most outstanding among the Masoretes was the family of ben Asher. In the tenth century of our era they produced the standard text that became the officially recognized text of the Hebrew Bible.

The ancient texts were written only in consonants, with a few letters to suggest certain important vowels. For example, the broad "A" at the end of words was often indicated by the letter *hē* (h). The names Sarah and Rebekah would be written simply SRH and RBQH in the Hebrew text. (Hebrew also lacks upper and lower case letters.) As Hebrew became less and less a spoken language, it became necessary to indicate the correct way to read the Scriptures in the synagogues.

Vowel Pointing

It was the Masoretes who developed the ingenious Hebrew phonetic system of dots and dashes to indicate not only full vowels, but even short vowels and half vowels. This is called vowel pointing. The quick little vowel that is heard in an English word like "nickel" was called a *shewa* by the

Masoretes. Their term has been adopted by phonetics experts to describe that sound in any language. (In some English dictionaries it is written as ə.) The Masoretic system is so clever and scientific that it makes modern English and French spelling seem paleolithic by comparison.

Kethîv *and* Qerē

These strange Aramaic words mean *written (kethîv)* and *read* or *called out (qerē)*. They are testimony to the great veneration that the Jews had for the Hebrew Bible. Even with the elaborate safeguards against error in copying—counting letters, knowing the central letter of each book, for example—mistakes did sometimes occur. When an obvious error was established, instead of *changing* the sacred text itself, a marginal note was given and a symbol was put over the offending *written* word to show the public reader how the word was to be *read.*

For example, over the centuries some words that were once acceptable became vulgar in usage and unsuitable for congregational reading. (See Chapter 8, "Something Blue" for some similar examples in the English KJV.) Deuteronomy 28:27 mentions hemorrhoids in the *kethîv* (written) text, but it was later considered an impolite term, so the marginal *qerē* (read text) changed it to *tumors.* Usually the KJV translators would go with the *qerē,* but here they chose to use the written text and translated it *emerod,* the older English form of *hemorrhoids.*

The Printed Texts

In 1611 the KJV translators had two printed Hebrew Bibles from which to translate, as well as some manuscripts, judging from certain marginal notes in the KJV. These Hebrew Bibles were extremely similar, since they were both edited from the text of ben Asher, considered to be the best representative of the Masoretic Bible. One of these texts was the Hebrew text of the Complutensian Polyglot (printed in 1514–17). The other was the standard Bible of the Jewish rabbis, the second edition of Daniel Bomberg, edited by Jacob ben Chayyim in 1525.

Other Old Testament Authorities

The KJV scholars relied primarily on the original languages, but they also made intelligent use of other sources, both Jewish and Christian. Miles Smith, one of the renowned "learned men" of 1611, says they were not negligent in consulting

> ...the translators or commentators, Chaldee, Hebrew, Syrian, Greek, or Latin, no nor Spanish, French, Italian, or Dutch .... But having and using helps as great as was needful, ... we have at the length, through the good hand of the Lord upon us, brought the work to pass that you now see.

Besides the Masoretic text itself the KJV translators also used the Masoretic *notes,* the ancient versions, Jewish tradition, and English Bible translation tradition.

Masoretic Notes

The margins of the Masoretes' Bibles are full of annotations called the *masorah magna* (great tradition) and the *masorah parva* (little tradition). The KJV scholars made good use of these notes.

Ancient Versions

Sometimes an early translation will have a reading that represents an ancient Hebrew text now lost, but apparently original. For example, Joshua 21:36, 37 is lacking in the Masoretic text. Yet the passage is found in the KJV because the missing verses were supplied from the Septuagint, Vulgate, and Syriac versions, as well as from the parallel passage in 1 Chronicles 6:63, 64. The NKJV Old Testament has many textual footnotes referring to these ancient versions.

In a scholarly paper presented to the Southern Region of the Evangelical Theological Society ("Textual Emendations in the Authorized Version"), Dr. James D. Price, Executive Old Testament Editor of the NKJV, evaluates the relative weight that the KJV learned men gave to the various versions:

> Four ancient versions were the most influential on the King James translators: (1) The Latin Vulgate was the one with which they were most conversant. This version had the greatest single influence on their emendations. (2) The Aramaic Targums seem to have had the second greatest influence. (3) The Greek Septuagint was the third most influential. (4) The

Syriac version had some influence, but seldom stood alone as the guide for an emendation. Other ancient and modern versions had no evident independent influence on emendations.[3]

Jewish Tradition

Although they were all Christians, the 1611 Hebraists were well versed in rabbinic studies, such as the Talmud and the commentaries of such Jewish scholars as Rashi, Eben Ezra, Kimchi, and Saadia Gāon. On rare occasions a deviation from the traditional Hebrew text in the KJV Old Testament seems to be based on one or more of these authorities. The NKJV footnotes include a few references to such Jewish traditions. Examples are found at Proverbs 8:30 and 30:31.

English Tradition

Since the KJV was not a new translation, but the repository of nearly a century of English Bible scholarship from Tyndale to the Douai (1526–1610), it was inevitable that some of the attractive phraseology that the king's men chose would be based on readings of their predecessors. Some of these readings may not have squared entirely with the Hebrew text.

An example in the KJV/NKJV is the word *dwell* in Psalm 23:6. The Hebrew reads *return,* but the difference is so slight, and the verse so famous, that it seemed not worth changing (RSV, NASB, and NIV also retain *dwell*).

Textual Emendations

Dr. Price categorizes the changes made by the 1611 translators as "justifiable emendations" and "unjustifiable emendations." Of the eighty-two he lists as justifiable Price writes: "Most were supported by evidence from the ancient versions. Some were made to harmonize the spelling of names or to harmonize parallel passages. Only five seem to have no ancient support."[4] He freely admits, however, that "not everyone will agree on the classification of individual emendations as justifiable and unjustifiable. In the less certain cases, differences in scholarly judgment are bound to arise."[5]

A clear example of such a justifiable emendation is in Psalm 24:4 where the *qerē* reads "My soul." This does not fit the context and has no ancient support. The *kethîv* is supported by some Hebrew manuscripts as well as the Septuagint, the Vulgate, and the Targum (cf. Exodus 20:7). All read "his soul," which fits the context perfectly.

Of the 146 emendations that Price considers unjustifiable, many have little or no support from ancient versions. Some merely have the support of rabbinic tradition.

An interesting example of the last category is in Genesis 36:24, where Anah found *water* (or hot springs) in the wilderness. This reading is in the Masoretic text and the Vulgate, but the KJV follows the Talmud (and Luther) which interprets it as *mules*. The Septuagint reads a proper name here, "Jamin," and the Targum reads "mighty men." Apparently even in ancient times there was a problem as to the word's meaning.

At least one emendation has messianic significance. In Psalm 22:16 the Masoretic text and the Targum read "Like a lion my hands and my feet," which makes little or no sense. Some Hebrew manuscripts, plus the Septuagint, Vulgate, and Syriac, read "they pierced My hands and My feet," which makes perfect sense in this psalm.[6]

The interesting examples chosen here are not typical. Most emendations are spelling variations, trivial details, and so forth. They are helpful, however, in countering the *excessive* veneration of the KJV to the point that it is treated as if *it,* and not the original manuscripts, were inspired. While the emendations of the KJV scholars seldom have serious effect on doctrine, they do show that the KJV, in it "unjustifiable emendations," is not infallible. The NKJV corrects these minor flaws.

Excessive Veneration of the King James Version

It is easy to criticize the Greek Orthodox Church for treating the Septuagint as more authoritative than the Hebrew original. After all, the *New* Testament was originally written in their delightful language! It is even easier for Protestants, at least, to fault the Roman Catholic Church for putting the Latin Vulgate on a higher level of authority than the inspired Hebrew and Greek. Both the Septuagint and the Vulgate are translations, *not the original.*

However, as much as we revere the KJV and wish to keep the standard Bible current, as our predecessors did (see Chapter 1, "A Firm Foundation"), some Protestants show a real danger of making a fetish of the KJV in the very same way.

In the same paper quoted above, Price warns of a certain modern departure from the Protestant doctrine of placing final authority in the original texts— *not in any version,* no matter how venerable and beautiful. He writes:

> This new doctrine has numerous flaws, one of which is the many emendations made to the Greek and Hebrew texts by the 1611 translators. In this context, an emendation is understood to be a failure to follow the

98

Greek or Hebrew text, whether the translators thought some other authority was superior to the Greek or Hebrew, or whether they were merely guilty of scholarly carelessness.[7]

He goes on to mention the 232 cases of emendation in the KJV Old Testament, some justifiable, as we have seen, and some not so justifiable. He states that while most changes do have some ancient support, some emendations "seem to have no verifiable ancient authority whatsoever."[8]

We conclude this section of our study with one final quotation from Dr. Price which is not intended to offend lovers of the King James Version (among whom we count ourselves), but to warn of a false doctrine of "double inspiration":

> These emendations cannot be justified on the basis of superior scholarly judgment of the 1611 translators; because there are equally competent scholars today, and textual-critical knowledge is more advanced. Nor can they be justified on the assumption that the 1611 translators received infallible divine guidance in their textual and translational decisions. This would amount to double inspiration, a departure from the historic doctrine. The divine inspiration of translators cannot be supported by Scripture. . . .[9]

Those who spent seven years laboring on the NKJV can vouch for the truth of Dr. Price's statement.

The Dead Sea Scrolls

Sometimes great discoveries spring from very trivial happenings. Such was the case with the so-called "Dead Sea Scrolls," which the celebrated archaeologist William F. Albright called "the greatest manuscript discovery of modern times." In the spring or early summer of 1947, a lost goat turned out to be the guide that led to a tremendous discovery for biblical scholarship.

Two Bedouin shepherds, searching for their lost goat in the desert region west of the Dead Sea, tossed a stone into a cave in the rocky escarpment high above them. To their surprise a crash resounded from the cave. They clambered up to investigate what had caused the noise and entered the cave. The rest is history.

Inside, the shepherds found eight big jars. From one of these they retrieved three large scrolls. The story of the attempts to sell them, and the final realization of scholars that they were ancient and very valuable Hebrew manuscripts, took some time. Professor John C. Trever, who was in Jerusalem at the time, photographed a scroll and sent the pictures to the American archaeologist, Dr. Albright.

Albright suggested a date of 50 B.C. for the scroll. This would make it about 1,000 years older than any Hebrew scroll then known to man. Later studies of coins, pottery, and palaeology (ancient script) confirmed a date between 175 B.C. and A.D. 68. So Albright was correct in his estimate.

The Dead Sea Scrolls are rather poorly named, since only a few of the manuscripts are still scrolls. Several other caves were explored and many thousands of fragments were retrieved, including previously unknown documents of a communal establishment at Qumran on the Dead Sea.

Parts of every book of the Hebrew Old Testament, except Esther, have been retrieved from the Dead Sea discoveries. The studies continue as a multinational and interfaith band of scholars keep sifting, sorting, piecing together, and translating the jigsaw puzzle of fragments.

Probably the most famous find was the Isaiah scroll, found in the first Qumran cave. It is a complete text of the great prophet. The remarkable thing is how very closely it resembles the text from which the KJV was made. The chief differences are in the spelling of certain types of words.

Many wild and sensational conjectures about the Qumran community and their scrolls have appeared in the popular press. But as the dust has settled, the main truth to come forth is that the Masoretic Text of the Old Testament has been very well preserved indeed.

The traditional Masoretic readings are still to be found in the text of the NKJV, even where the Dead Sea Scrolls differ, but important variant readings from Qumran will be found in the notes.

NOTES

[1]Modern Jewish people like to refer to their Bible as the "*Tanach*." This is an acronym formed from the first letters of the Hebrew words for the three divisions of the Old Testament in the Jewish order: *Torah* (Law), N*evîîm* (Prophets), and K*etûvîm* (Writings). Vowels are added to make the word pronounceable.

[2]From Moses (ca. 1400 B.C.) to Malachi (ca. 400 B.C.) is about a thousand years.

[3]James D. Price, "Textual Emendations in the Authorized Version," a paper presented to the Southern Region of the Evangelical Theological Society, March 22, 1986, p. 5. Dr. Price has graciously allowed free use of his typically meticulous seventy-eight-page work in writing this chapter.

[4]Ibid., p. 7.

[5]Ibid., footnote 6.

[6]Since the Masoretes were post-Christian in time, one is tempted to wonder if the text was changed on purpose to avoid a strong messianic prophecy of the crucifixion.

[7]Price, "Textual Emendations," p. 1.

[8]Ibid., p. 2.

[9]Ibid.

10

Complete New Testament Textual Data

My first brush with what is called "textual criticism"—the art and science of determining the *exact original wording* of an ancient text—was in high school. It was *New Testament* textual criticism, for me the most important kind. Of course Anacostia High in Washington, D.C. didn't have a course in textual criticism, even though it was a very good school, complete with fine teachers, ivy covered pillars, and exchange students from several foreign countries.

It was in the happy days of old (the fabulous 50s!) when we were still allowed to read the Bible and pray in public schools. Every morning over the loudspeaker system a chapter or long paragraph was read from the Bible. Then Protestant, Catholic, and Jewish kids would join together in reciting the Lord's Prayer. Frankly, I think it helped the attitude of a lot of students. I know it helped me.

One day two or three very amiable students transferred from D.C. parochial schools to our school. They, too, had been saying the Lord's Prayer for years in their school. But it was in the Douai Version, not the KJV. And they weren't about to "switch brands," though the prayers are nearly identical— except for one significant detail.

As we came near the end of the prayer, these two or three guys would say *very loudly,* ". . . but deliver us from evil, AMEN!" The rest of the class went on with the familiar ending of the Protestant Bible:

"For thine is the kingdom,
and the power,
and the glory, for ever,
amen."

As this behavior went on from day to day I got the message: The Douai Version of the Bible had a shorter text of the Lord's Prayer than the KJV. My father (educated in a Norwegian Lutheran school) had taught me, quite accurately, that the Reformation had deleted and trimmed down many things from the Middle Ages that the Reformers felt were inconsistent with the New Testament faith. But here was a case of Rome having a less elaborate "liturgy" than Canterbury, Wittenburg, or Geneva!

Most modern Protestant Bibles—such as the RSV, NEB, and NIV—now conform to the Latin Vulgate in this detail and to those manuscripts upon which it is based. It is not a *doctrinal* difference. All Christians believe that Matthew 6:13b is *true,* but some don't believe it is part of the original text. It is a *textual* matter.

The King James Bible was translated from printed Greek texts based on manuscripts that *contained* Matthew 6:13. The Latin Vulgate, the official version of the Church of Rome, was made from manuscripts that *lacked* it. Until fairly modern times most Roman Catholic Bibles were made from the *Latin,* like Knox's very literary translation, in the light of the original languages. Modern Catholic Bibles[1] are from the original Greek and Hebrew.

The omission or retention of the ending on the Lord's Prayer is a clear and dramatic illustration of what we mean by *completeness* in the text of the NKJV. Most textual matters are far less well known, less noticeable, and less important. But if we believe that the Bible is God's Word, no reading, however short, should be allowed to "fall through the cracks," as they say, unless we are very sure that it is not a part of the inspired text.

Even more basic than translation is the text from which any translation is made. For example, the inclusion or omission of a word, phrase, clause, sentence, or in just two cases in the New Testament a whole paragraph,[2] is not a matter of how loose or how literal a translation is to be, but of the text from which one is translating.

Fortunately, the text of the New Testament is very well established. This must be stressed before examining the different theories on the variants that do occur in the manuscripts and how important they may be.

The Area of Fact

First of all, everyone who has been introduced to the subject of New Testament textual criticism (the science of recovering the precise wording of the original where it may vary in some manuscripts) is aware that the manuscript materials are very plentiful.

The Greek Manuscripts

There are over five thousand manuscripts of the Greek New Testament, although only one manuscript contains a whole Testament. This number is far greater than the number of manuscripts supporting the Greek and Latin classics, some of which have a mere handful of ancient manuscripts. The Greek manuscripts of the New Testament were written very soon after the writing of the original texts. The manuscripts are from various parts of the ancient world—Palestine, Asia Minor, Egypt, and the West.

Because so much has been said about textual variants, many people have received the impression that the New Testament is on shaky ground. Not so! Fully eighty-five percent of the text is the same in all types of manuscripts. As for the other fifteen percent, we should point out that much of the material concerns details that do not even show up in an English translation. Such things as word order, spelling, and slightly variant forms of some verbs seldom are reproduced in translation.

Most of the variations are caused by accidental copyists' errors. However, with all the heretical groups seeking to corrupt orthodox Christian doctrine (such as the Gnostics against whom Paul wrote in Colossians and John in his First Epistle), we would be naive to think that no changes were made intentionally in the interest of some heterodox cult or sect.

Of the approximately five thousand manuscripts there are four categories of writing and material used.

The Papyri. The oldest manuscripts, usually quite fragmentary, were written on papyrus in capital letters. There are over eighty papyrus manuscripts, most of which are in codex (book) form, but four are fragments from scrolls. The papyri are designated by the letter "p" with a superscripted number. The earliest uncontested known New Testament fragment (Rylands papyrus 52) is dated only about three decades after the death of the Apostle John. It contains several verses from John 18.

The Uncials. The word *uncial,* from the Latin word for "inch," is used to describe these manuscripts because of the large capital[3] letters that are used. There are about 260 uncial manuscipts, only one of which contains the entire New Testament. Nevertheless, every New Testament book has ample uncial witnesses. The uncials are designated by English and Greek capital letters. One uncial manuscript, Codex Sinaiticus, is designated by the Hebrew letter *Aleph.*

The Minuscules. There are about 2,700 minuscules. The minuscules are written in smaller letters in a slanted and flowing ("cursive") script. Most of these are from later centuries and contain the Byzantine text. It was from a half-dozen late minuscules that Erasmus produced his first edition of the Greek New Testament in 1516.

Lectionaries. Greek lectionaries are similar to the Scriptures seen in the

Book of Common Prayer, with special readings for Sunday and church feast days. They are, of course, in the original language, and still used by the Greek Orthodox Church.

In summary, the Greek New Testament is supported by thousands of manuscripts from many different parts of the ancient Roman Empire. They generally agree on most points, from the earliest papyrus manuscripts down to the late Byzantine ones.

The Church Fathers

In addition, there are thousands of quotations from the Greek New Testament in the church fathers. These fathers lived from the second century until early medieval times, but the manuscripts containing their works trace back only from about the fourth century on. If the actual manuscripts of the New Testament were lost, virtually the entire book could be recovered from these quotations.

The Versions

In addition to Greek materials there are manuscripts in several languages other than Greek, such as Latin, Syriac, and Coptic. At the very least they tell us whether a certain phrase existed in the Greek manuscripts from which they were translated. Usually they tell us much more.

The Traditional Greek Text (Textus Receptus)

The manuscripts of the Greek New Testament available to the earlier European scholars were primarily late medieval copies that spread across Europe after Constantinople fell to the Muslims in 1453. These were Bible manuscripts used by the Greek-speaking church, arriving just in time for the newly awakened Renaissance and Reformation interest in studying Greek, and also for the newly invented art of printing.

Before the Reformation the Western (European) church had shown very little interest in the Greek Bible, since Latin was Rome's liturgical language, and the Latin Vulgate was her authoritative Bible. Consequently, there were few Greek Bibles in the West before 1453, except for a few very old ones in the archives of some libraries.

When the Dutch scholar Desiderius Erasmus (1469–1536) published the first Greek New Testament in 1516,[4] he had just a few late manuscripts with which to work. Later editions of the Greek Testament were also based on similar manuscripts. So, apart from minor variations, all the early printed editions are essentially the same.

The Greek New Testaments used by the King James translators other than Erasmus' texts included the Complutensian Polyglot printed in 1514 (but not published till 1520), Stephanus' texts, and Beza's texts. "The editions of Beza, particularly that of 1598, and the two last editions of Stevens were the chief sources used for the English Authorized Version of 1611."[5]

The Elzivir brothers of the Netherlands published several editions of the Greek New Testament with essentially the same text as that of Erasmus, Beza, and Stephanus. In the Latin introduction to the 1633 edition, Elzivir stated that this text was the "*textum ab omnibus receptum*" ("text received by all"). This was shortened to "Textus Receptus," and was later applied to Stephanus' text of 1550. This name was also applied in a general way to all texts of the Byzantine type. The traditional Greek text has been called the *Textus Receptus* ever since that time.

The Area of Theory

Until the nineteenth century the Greek texts used by Bible translators were fairly uniform, being based on ancient manuscripts that were in substantial agreement. As a result, there were few questions raised concerning the conformity of the then current Greek texts to the original autographs written by the hands of the evangelists and apostles.

But in the nineteenth century many earlier manuscripts of the Greek New Testament were discovered that caused some Bible scholars to change their approach toward evaluating the Greek text. This was important for Bible translating because the text of the older manuscripts was somewhat different from the Textus Receptus in a number of places. Simply because of their antiquity many scholars regarded them as better copies of the original autographs and thus more authoritative than the later manuscripts on which the Textus Receptus was based.

The nineteenth-century discovery of these manuscripts, differing somewhat from the traditional text, caused scholars to consider how to determine which differing readings were original and which were later changes. The methods applied to classical Latin and Greek texts were not satisfactory. Finally, many accepted a theory developed by Fenton John Anthony Hort and Brooke Foss Westcott. These authors propounded their theory in their two-volume work published in 1881, *The New Testament in the Original Greek.*

The Westcott-Hort Theory

Westcott and Hort advocated that genealogical relationships among manuscripts were of primary importance, and that the evidence from kinds of texts ("texttypes") thus identified should be evaluated on the basis of how often a particular texttype is found to be correct. Thus a texttype that has the reputation for being correct most often should be given more weight as a witness than one that is frequently wrong. On the basis of their investigation they identified four principle texttypes which they called the *Syrian*, the *Western*, the *Alexandrian*, and the *Neutral*.

The text they regarded as the latest and least reliable they called "Syrian," but it is generally called "Byzantine" today. It is the type from which the text of Erasmus was made and that lies behind the King James and all early translations. The very smoothness and completeness of the text led these scholars to believe it was late, edited, and hence corrupt. Hort taught that the text is in such a vast majority of extant manuscipts because the Byzantine Church made it their official text. There is no historical evidence for this, however.

Westcott and Hort's favored text they called "Neutral," a name now rejected as too biased. This is the text heavily dependent on *Codex Vaticanus,* their very favorite early manuscript, and *Codex Sinaiticus,* their second most favored text.

Some scholars, however, were disturbed that a mere handful of recently discovered manuscripts (often from three to five percent), no matter how much older, should be made to counterbalance the hundreds of years of reliance on the traditional text and the overwhelming multitude of manuscripts supporting it.

The most outspoken of these was John W. Burgon, Dean of Chichester. He favored the Byzantine text (Westcott and Hort's "Syrian") because it is supported by the vast majority of manuscripts. He regarded Codex Vaticanus and Codex Sinaiticus as corrupt and unreliable as witnesses to the original text. Instead he favored the witness of the early church fathers and versions, asserting that these witnesses supported the Byzantine text, which is essentially the Textus Receptus.[6]

The Critical Text Theory

In more recent times textual scholars have classified the manuscripts into different texttypes from those of Westcott and Hort. They have also departed from such extreme dependence on Sinaiticus (*Aleph*) and Vaticanus (*B*), giving more weight to other early witnesses, such as the papyri. Many scholars are willing to include the Byzantine text in their formula rather than totally ignore this large segment of evidence. In addition to this, modern scholars choose the reading they think best fits the context, and according to what they believe a copyist would be most likely to write. Thus they produce what is essentially an "eclectic text," that is, one based on choosing individual readings rather than following a certain textual theory. The resultant text, often called the "critical text," is used in most modern translations of the New Testament. It is not markedly different from the Westcott-Hort text, but has a wider base.

The Majority Text Theory

There has been a recent resurgence of the conviction that the Divine preservation of the text of the New Testament can best be discovered in the type of text used in Greek-speaking churches as far back as we can trace, and also into modern times. This is the text found in fully eighty to ninety-five percent of the manuscripts. It is similar to the text John Burgon advocated, and, except in Revelation, to the Textus Receptus (from which the King James was made).[7] In Revelation the majority text is twice as likely to agree with the critical text as with the TR when there are textual variants.[8]

A variant that first appeared in a fourth-century manuscript, when hundreds of manuscripts reflecting the true reading of the original were already in circulation, would have had a poor chance of becoming the dominant reading. For example, Codex Vaticanus, a fourth-century manuscript, has very few descendants. Majority-text supporters use this as one argument for choosing the text based on the vast bulk of manuscripts.

I used to illustrate the majority-text position to my Greek class in the following way: I would ask for a show of hands of those students who had British last names—English, Scottish, Irish, or Welsh. A very large percentage of hands would go up. Then I would ask for a show of hands of those who had Slavic names—Polish, Russian, Czech, and so forth. Usually only two or three hands would go up.

"While people don't reproduce exactly like manuscripts," I would say, "the principle is the same. The British reached North America early and had very large families, whose children also had large families, and so on. In the nineteenth century came the Russians, Poles, and so forth. There is no way that Slavic Americans could ever overtake the British Americans in numbers."

Similarly, the readings found in the largest number of manuscripts are most likely to trace back to the earliest copies—the autographs actually penned by the evangelists and apostles themselves. These would have time to multiply the most.

It is also worth noting that most of the autographs were originally sent to and carefully preserved by churches in what later became the Byzantine Empire—in Corinth, Galatia, Ephesus, Philippi, Colosse, Thessalonica, and other places. As far as we know, not a single original autograph of a Gospel or Epistle was ever sent to Egypt, the country of origin of Codex Vaticanus and Codex Sinaiticus.

The main argument against the majority text is that none of our earliest (e.g., Vaticanus, Sinaiticus) manuscripts are of this type. The majority-text response is that the papyri found in Egypt during the nineteenth century are corrupt copies of much earlier manuscripts, whose originals had been sent to Asia Minor and Europe. The major manuscripts we have from Egypt (e.g., Vaticanus, Sinaiticus) survived because of disuse and dry climate.

Although it used to be said that no Byzantine readings were ancient, early papyri have been found more recently which do contain such formerly condemned, so-called "late" readings.

The NKJV Position

Most current New Testaments use some modification of the Westcott-Hort text, such as an eclectic one not too far removed from that text. Seminary and college professors especially are surprised that the NKJV used such a conservative text as the Textus Receptus.[9]

We decided to stick to this venerable Reformation era Greek text for two reasons:

First, the NKJV is an update of an historic version translated from a specific type of text. We felt it was unwise to change the base from which it was made. As noted earlier, the translators of the English Revised Version of the New Testament (1881) were soundly criticized for slipping in the Westcott-Hort Greek text when it was not part of their mandate from the church.

Secondly, in recent years the extreme reliance on a handful of our oldest manuscripts—all necessarily from Egypt—has decreased. There is a greater openness to giving the so-called Byzantine manuscripts a fair hearing. For example, Dr. Harry Sturz, our late colleague on the New Testament Executive Review Committee, wrote a scholarly book showing how these manuscripts are worthy of study, not total neglect.[10]

Actually, the NKJV textual policy in the New Testament is more objective than that in any modern version of which we are aware. Translators of most contemporary versions assume that the currently popular view is correct, and they often label those readings supporting that theory as "the best manuscripts." Also, manuscripts supporting the KJV-type reading are largely ignored. Since these latter readings almost always reflect the readings of eighty percent of the extant manuscripts, and very frequently close to ninety-five percent of the manuscripts, this labeling policy seems a bit unbalanced.

The NKJV Textual Notes

On every page of the NKJV New Testament the studious reader will find three different textual views represented.

1. The text of the New King James New Testament itself is the traditional one used by Luther and Calvin, as well as by such Catholic scholars as Erasmus, who produced it. Later (1633) it was called the *Textus Receptus,* or "TR."

Very few scholars would today support this text exactly as it stands, but it certainly is not the corrupt and "villainous" thing that F. J. A. Hort vowed to destroy when he was twenty-three years old.[11]

2. "NU" in the NKJV notes stands for the *critical text,* based on Westcott-Hort, but with other selected readings as well. NU stands for *N*estle-Aland and *U*nited Bible Societies, whose Greek texts are virtually identical. However, their "apparatuses" (sets of footnotes detailing variant readings) are different. This is the preference of a majority of present-day scholars, but not of the majority of the manuscripts.

3. "M" in the notes stands for the *majority text.* It is close to the TR, except in Revelation. However, those TR readings that have weak support, such as 1 John 5:7, 8, are corrected. This text is available in print as *The Greek New Testament According to the Majority Text* (see Bibliography).

Thus, there is a greater selection of textual material in the NKJV footnotes than in most other English versions. A good example of all three options occurring in one verse is Acts 5:41:

> "So they departed from the presence of the council, rejoicing that they were counted worthy to suffer shame for <u>His name</u>" (Acts 5:41).

The NKJV footnote reads: "NU-Text reads *the name;* M-Text reads *the name of Jesus.*" Thus interesting textual variants are cited carefully with their general source for comparison and study. F. F. Bruce praises the NKJV on this very point:

> . . . the textual notes are specially helpful, indicating not only where the wording differs from that of the generally accepted critical text but also where it differs from the majority text. These notes make no value judgments but enable the reader to see at a glance what the textual situation is and to assess it in the light of the context.[12]

No matter what one's viewpoint is on this difficult subject, there is enough material in the NKJV footnotes on the New Testament manuscript variations for the vast majority of Bible students. If more detailed studies are desired, the apparatuses to the Greek New Testaments must be consulted.

Two Crucial Paragraphs

As we have noted, the Greek text of the New Testament is well preserved, widely supported by Greek manuscripts and ancient versions, and differs chiefly in little details, many of which are too small to show up in translation. These include word order, spelling, slight variations in verb tenses or in the definite article.

There are, however, two complete paragraphs whose authenticity is widely called into question. Many modern Bibles set these paragraphs off by brackets, a white space, and/or a line to show that the translators or editors reject or at least question them. Since both are of real theological significance, and both are printed in the NKJV as part of the sacred text, an explanation is in order.

The Resurrection—Mark 16:9-20

The New American Standard Bible (1971) puts this paragraph in brackets and has a note reading "Some of the oldest manuscripts omit from verse 9 through 20." The version adds an alternate proposed reading for the end of the book, stating that this reading is found in "a few later manuscripts and versions."

These notes are misleading. The "Some of the oldest manuscripts" are really just *two* Greek manuscripts (there is also one much later manuscript). It should be said that the "sacred and imperishable proclamation" (shorter ending of Mark) also has very little to commend its authenticity.

The note in the New International Version is more accurate as to *number* of manuscripts, but highly interpretive: "The two most reliable early manuscripts do not have Mark 16:9-20." Actually, the reliability of Vaticanus and Sinaiticus is strictly a theory, though widely taught.

Also, one of these two manuscripts contain space for the missing paragraph, a very unusual thing when using expensive vellum (fine animal skins). Apparently the scribe was aware of the passage but lacked it in his exemplar. The other manuscript shows evidence of having been tampered with to fill up the space.

It is common to say that the style of Mark 16:9-20 is unlike Mark's, but this is subjective.[13] Actually, there are stylistic parallels between Mark 16 and Mark 1.

Verse 8 of chapter 16 (where the two minority manuscripts close) ends with the little word *gar* ("for") in Greek, which is usually the second word in a sentence. To end a book on this word seems most unlikely.

Also, especially if one accepts the theory that Mark is the oldest Gospel, we would have the Resurrection story ending without the risen Christ actually appearing—a disappointing Easter indeed!

Some try to solve the problem by saying that the original ending is lost and verses 9-20 are a makeshift substitute. This seems a very weak theory in light of our Lord's promise that His words would never pass away (Matthew 24:35).

Frankly, one fears that some would like to be rid of the passage because of verses 16-18 on the doctrines of baptism and miracles.

The point that the footnotes in most Bibles fail to report is that 1,400 manuscripts do contain this passage. Further, St. Jerome, when he translated the New Testament into Latin, included Mark 16:9-20. It is significant that he did so in the fourth century, when the dissenting Egyptian manuscripts were also written! Apparently these two copies which lacked this passage were not representative in their own time.

In short, the long ending of Mark is on a firm foundation and widely supported. The NKJV footnotes alert the reader to the problem without telling him what is best.

The Adulterous Woman Forgiven—John 7:53—8:11

Even people who feel this wasn't written by John generally admit it is an authentic story. It rings true. One excellent professor once told us in Greek class that he believed it was true and authentic, but probably not part of John, so he wouldn't preach from it. Recently hearing a tape of one of his sermons on the radio I was happy to hear him preaching from it.

The manuscript evidence for this story is not nearly as strong as for Mark 16, but as far back as 1913 there were 900 Greek copies of John that did contain it, *and many more are known to exist today.*

The NIV note says, "The earliest and most reliable manuscripts do not have John 7:53—8:11." Let it be emphasized again that the *earliest* Greek copies of John—those from Egypt—do indeed lack this text, but their superior reliability is only a theory.

St. Augustine wrote that the paragraph was excised for fear it would promote immorality. The gracious forgiveness of our Lord in the passage certainly does contrast sharply with the harsh legalistic rituals that Christendom evolved for an adulterer to get back into communion.

The argument that the style is not like John's is subjective and has been well answered by Zane C. Hodges in articles in *Bibliotheca Sacra*.[14] The

Introduction to *The New Testament According to the Majority Text* gives a detailed technical defense of the passage (pp. xxiii–xxxii).

Perhaps the best way for the Bible reader to test the passage is to read John 7:52, skip over 7:53 through 8:11 to verse 12, and see if it hangs together well. It does not! The NIV obscures this *non sequitur* by supplying the word "people" to the text of 8:12. Every Greek text says "them," and if 7:53 were the verse right before it, the "them" would refer to the meeting of Nicodemus and the Sanhedrin. *But our Lord was not at that meeting.*

A person can use the NKJV, just as millions have used the KJV, without agreeing with the inclusion or exclusion of every disputed word or even these two paragraphs. None of the three traditions on every page of the New Testament—*Textus Receptus, critical, or majority text,* is labeled "best" or "most reliable." The reader is permitted to make up his or her own mind about the correct reading.

Since I have made a special study of these textual issues,[15] I trust the strong defense of our textual policy will not offend those who differ, and as I well know, do so in good faith.

Textual Criticism and Inerrancy

If the New Testament is essentially so well documented and reliable, why all the controversy? The reason is that these twenty-seven books are not merely an historic monument of "early Christian literature," but God's Word written to His people—our daily guide. As such we care even about the "jots and tittles," even where they may not affect any doctrine. Actually, most Christian doctrines are unchallenged by these variant readings, but it is true that some doctrines are more weakly (and others more strongly) supported in certain texts.

One major teaching that is effectively negated if one follows the *critical* text is the doctrine of inerrancy. This is the view that there are *no* actual errors in the original manuscripts, though there are copyists' mistakes. This is the belief of the teams that produced the NKJV.

For example, in his scholarly article in the *The Journal of the Evangelical Theological Society,* Dr. James Borland points out that the critical text contains at least the following two historical errors.[16]

Nonexistent Judean Kings

In Matthew 1:7 and 10 two non-existent kings are listed in the genealogy of our Lord: Amos and Asaph. There was a prophet Amos and a musician named Asaph, but the kings in question were *Amon* and *Asa*.

Someone who believes God's Word can contain errors could say (and some do) that Matthew was in error and he was corrected by later scribes. Even if there were no inspiration, such a meticulous writer as Matthew simply *would not* make such an error in the history of his own people; and for those of us who believe in inerrancy, he *could not* make it.

Theologically conservative translations that use the critical text, such as the NASB and the NIV, choose to depart from their text here—with good reason!

A Scientifically Impossible Eclipse

Even more serious, as Borland points out, is the scientific error in the critical text of Luke 23:45. The overwhelming majority of manuscripts read with the TR and the majority text that "the sun was darkened" (Greek *eskotisthē*). A handful of ancient Egyptian manuscripts read "the sun being eclipsed" (*eklipontos*). This is impossible. Christ's death took place at Passover when the moon is full. There is no way that the sun can be eclipsed at that time. God caused the sun to be "darkened" by means not disclosed. The talented (and liberal) translator James Moffatt actually imputes this scientific error to St. Luke in his version.

The Kingdom and the Power and the Glory

We started this somewhat controversial chapter with a teenager's experience with the Lord's Prayer. What better way to end it than with the same model prayer?

Some scholars say that the early Christians added the ending in Matthew 6:13b to make the prayer liturgically more polished. After all, it is traditional to end a Jewish prayer with God, not evil—or worse, the evil one! Since the contents are similar to wording in 1 Chronicles 29:11, this text has been suggested as the source of the ending.

I think there is a better solution! Just as the Virgin Mary's Magnificat is full of scriptural allusions, not as some sort of "redaction," but flowing in a most natural way, so her divine Son's model prayer expresses the overflow, humanly speaking, of a mind steeped in God's Word. I suggest that His prayer was perfectly complete—and completely perfect—when it first fell from the lips of our Lord:

"For Yours is the kingdom
and the power
and the glory forever.
Amen."[17]

NOTES

[1]Such as *The New American Bible* or *The Jerusalem Bible.*

[2]Mark 16:9-20 and John 7:53—8:11; see discussion below.

[3]Technically there were no capitals at that time. As the "lower case" or "small" letters evolved in later centuries, the original letters became "capital" letters.

[4]The first *printed* Greek New Testament (1514) waited for papal approval until 1520 to be *published.*

[5]*The New Testament: The Greek Text Underlying the English Authorized Version of 1611* (London: The Trinitarian Bible Society, [n.d.]), preface.

[6]John W. Burgon, *The Traditional Text of the Holy Gospels Vindicated and Established,* arranged, completed, and edited by Edward Miller (London: George Bell and Sons, 1896).

[7]In 1988 the Majority Text Society was formed (Box 860639, Plano, Texas, 75086-0639). Wilbur Pickering (Ph.D. in linguistics, University of Toronto) was elected first president. See Bibliography for his book on textual criticism.

[8]Probably the reason the *Textus Receptus* is so unrepresentative of the manuscript tradition of Revelation is the fact that Erasmus had only one faulty manuscript of that book. It even lacked the last six verses. In his desire to be first to publish a Greek New Testament Erasmus translated these missing verses into Greek from the Latin!

[9]Earlier, it was planned to use the majority text as the translation base for the NKJV New Testament. But deeper reflection led us to adhere to the traditional King James text and to reflect the majority text (M) in the notes along with the critical text (NU).

[10]Harry A. Sturz, *The Byzantine Text-Type and New Testament Textual Criticism* (Nashville: Thomas Nelson Publishers, 1984).

[11]F. J. A. Hort, *Life and Letters of Fenton John Anthony Hort,* 2 vols., (London: MacMillan and Co., 1881), I:211.

[12]Quoted from Thomas Nelson brochure, "New King James—the Accurate One."

[13]Read the "shorter ending" of Mark in the NASB and you will see a clear and almost blatant difference in style.

[14]See Hodges' two articles on "The Woman Taken in Adultery" in the Bibliography under Periodicals.

[15]In three fine schools I was strongly taught the critical theory, and only after graduating from seminary did I come to study textual criticism for myself. The culmination of all this was my conversion to the majority text position and later to being asked to co-edit a Greek New Testament (see Bibliography under Zane C. Hodges).

[16]James Borland, "Re-examining Textual-Critical Principles and Practices Used to Negate Inerrancy," *Journal of the Evangelical Theological Society,* Vol. 25, December, 1982, pp. 499-506.

[17]Since most manuscripts do contain the ending, isn't it easier for Christians to believe that some manuscripts dropped off the ending simply by careless copying?

11

Complete Equivalence in Translation

So far in our studies of the New King James Version we have seen in the first part of the book the great importance of *accuracy* in communicating God's Word to today's reader of English. This consists of building on the excellent work of our predecessors and bringing their work up to date with new findings and changes in our language.

Next we surveyed the *beauty* of the Tyndale-King James tradition and how we sought to retain and even enhance that beauty where possible. Much of the Bible's beauty was seen largely to emerge from the original texts themselves, not from the genius of the translators.

In this third and last section of the book we have talked of the necessity of providing relatively *complete* data (for a translation) regarding both the Old and New Testament texts.

The area of controversy is the New Testament text, though even that was seen as firmly established except for a small part of the text. As to this small area of disagreement, the decision of the teams that produced the NKJV was to retain the traditional text rather than to delete or change material that lays claim to being part of the inspired Word. However, the rather full notes that present both of two alternative positions—the critical and majority texts—give the interested reader variant readings of significance. Also, rather than labeling any of them as "best" or "most reliable" (which is a question of theoretical interpretation) we classify them as to the school of thought which prefers these readings.

As we sum up the contribution of the New King James Version as a standard Bible, we would like to propose our basic theory of translation. This is most important.

Dr. James Price, an expert in the area of linguistics, in his booklet *Complete Equivalence in Bible Translation,* writes:

> A translation is no better than the theory on which it is based. A sound translation theory produces a sound translation. Yet Bible translators are

not agreed on what constitutes "sound translation theory" for Bible translation. The disagreement centers on how much of the original language structure can be represented in the receiving language without decreasing either the accuracy or understandability of the translation.[1]

The solution to the problem of whether to stress the original language from which one is translating or the "receptor" language into which the original is being rendered, has spawned translations as rigid as an interlinear at one extreme (stressing the original) to a loose paraphrase on the other (stressing the receptor language). There are several shades of translation theory in between.

Since no one has proposed that an interlinear should be used for a *standard* Bible, we will not include it in our discussion. We will examine the handful of translation theories that are widely recommended today.

Literal Translation

The oldest and most traditional method of translation seeks to follow the structure and wording of the original language wherever the receptor language allows, and to be more free and idiomatic where a literal rendering would be misleading or confusing.

Nearly all of the famous versions of Judeo-Christian history fall into this category: the Septuagint, the Vulgate, Luther's German Bible, Tyndale and its revisions, down to the KJV and its later revisions.

Some of these revisions (such as the English Revised Version of 1885 and the U.S. counterpart, the American Standard Version of 1901) go too far in their literal renderings. They have been rightly criticized for being too rigid and have even been called "school-boy" translations. They have been a favorite with Greek and Hebrew students for that very reason, often much to the chagrin of their professors!

The King James Version is actually more idiomatic than either of these later revisions, and also is in much better English style.

Those who criticize the literal method tend to agree with Eugene Glassman's description of it:

> Those who follow this [literal] method assume that languages are largely alike, at least enough so that a translator can move directly from one language to another. The approach is generally called *formal correspondence,* in which the word *formal* is used in the sense of being concerned with the outward *form* of something as distinguished from its content. In other words, the emphasis is on the form of the original or source language, with the assumption that the form can largely be carried across into the new or receptor language.[2]

Especially bad examples are usually chosen to show the failings of the literal method.

The question remains, though: Why did the Septuagint, the Vulgate, the Luther Bible, and the Authorized Version have such magnificent spiritual and literary harvests if their method of translation was so faulty?

Paraphrase

On a fairly recent national television interview on today's Bible translations, the proponent of one of the most popular paraphrases said, "There's no real difference between translation and paraphrase."

We beg to differ! Granted that there are some translations on the border between translation and paraphrase, the theory, practice, and results are really quite different.

A paraphrase takes great liberties in word order: adding words and phrases, rewriting, and altering the style. Because of this freedom of rendering, the translator has a great deal of opportunity (and temptation) to inject his own interpretations into the text even if he seeks to be objective.

An example of this can be seen in comparing the literal rendering of Acts 13:48 with the *Living Bible's* paraphrase:

When the Gentiles heard this, they were very glad and rejoiced in Paul's message; and as many as wanted eternal life, believed (LB).	Now when the Gentiles heard this, they were glad and glorified the word of the Lord. And as many as had been appointed to eternal life believed (NKJV).

First of all "the word of the Lord" is a much broader term than "Paul's message," because even the great apostle to the Gentiles didn't have *all* of God's truth.

More serious is the rendering of the verb explaining why these people believed. Theologically, both things are true—God's appointment and man's desire to be saved. But the question is, "What did Luke write?" By no stretch of the imagination can the passive voice of the Greek verb here[3] mean "wanted" or even the first alternative in the Living Bible's margin, "were disposed to." The second Living Bible alternative, "ordained to," is accurate (it's the KJV rendering), but today it suggests church ordination, so the simpler and quite literal "appointed to" of the NKJV is clearer.

Paraphrases have their place. They are useful for rapid reading of a book to get the sweep of the content. They are not accurate enough for doctrinal studies or standard church uses, such as memorization and public worship.

Expanded Translation

Since many words can have more than one meaning, and Greek words often have subtle shades of meaning that are difficult to transmit in a strictly literal translation, some translators seek to insert extra words, explanatory comments, and paraphrases of verb tenses. Wuest's *Expanded Translation* and *The Amplified Bible* are popular examples of this method.

One of the main problems with this type of version is that it gives the impression to one who doesn't know Greek or Hebrew that the text is very fluid and uncertain in meaning. While it is true that many words can have a number of meanings when they appear on a list, *in context,* the precise meaning of a word is generally pinned down rather successfully.

As to the readability and literary value of works produced by this method of translation, Price comments:

> The result is complex, wordy, often hard to understand, lacking any literary beauty. Such work is actually a running commentary, the author's interpretation, not a translation. Expanded translations may be helpful for study purposes, but they confuse those who cannot distinguish what part of the translation comes from the original language, and what part comes from the translator. The multiplicity of meanings may lead to doctrinal error.[4]

Dynamic Equivalence

Dynamic equivalence is a modern method of translation that basically amounts to scientific paraphrase. While it often totally restructures the text to fit the receptor language (the one into which one is translating), ideally it does so according to scientific principles.

The Ideals of Dynamic Equivalence

The goals of the method are high, namely

> to produce in the reader or hearer in the receptor language the same reaction to the message that the original author sought to produce in the immediate readers or listeners. It assumes that the original message was natural and meaningful and that the grammatical structure and words were not discouragingly difficult but that people used them in their everyday lives.[5]

Those who seek dynamic equivalence in translation attempt to produce in the receptor language the closest natural equivalent of the message contained in the source language, keeping in mind both the meaning and the style. They recognize, of course, that no translation can succeed one hundred per cent; every translation suffers some loss of information, some addition of information, and possibly also some distortion of information. For all that, however, one can find the closest equivalent possible.[6]

The method is too complex to review here in detail.[7]

Suffice it to say that the original text is subjected to *analysis,* the information is *transferred* to the receptor language, various *adjustments* are made, and the whole text is *restructured* to fit the new language.

If done with extreme care and by translators who know both *linguistics* and sound *theology,* the results can be very helpful, especially in languages that are very different from Hebrew and Greek. (English and Greek are both Indo-European languages and have much in common. Hebrew also translates nicely into English without major restructuring.)

The Problems of Dynamic Equivalence

The problem with dynamic equivalence is the area of subjectivity in the transfer of information to the receptor language. Glassman admits this:

Transfer is essentially a subjective process that goes on in the minds of translators as they struggle in their roles as "bridge" between the meanings of the source language and the various options open to them in expressing that meaning in the receptor language.[8]

As in ordinary paraphrase, there is too much opportunity to introduce interpretive material into the receptor language.

Also, on the other hand, such expressions as "and," "behold," "it came to pass," and so forth tend to be freely eliminated in dynamic-equivalence translations of the Old Testament.

In languages that have no passive voice, for example, an expression such as "they shall be called the sons of God" (Matthew 5:9) has to be put in the active voice: "[Someone] will call them the children of God." Whether it is God, other people, or both is not specified by our Lord. English does have the passive voice and therefore a dynamic-equivalence rendering such as the New English Bible's (NEB) "God shall call them his sons" is unnecessarily interpretive.

Such a literal translation as the New American Standard Bible's (NASB) "covenant and lovingkindness" (Nehemiah 1:5) or "covenant and mercy"

(NKJV) contains two items, following the Hebrew. Sometimes two items, one subordinate to the other, just constitute a literary way of saying one thing.⁹

Dynamic-equivalence translations such as the Jerusalem Bible (JB) read "covenant of faithful love" or "covenant of love" (NIV).

In the first place the word they translate as "love" is quoted in the New Testament as "mercy" even by the JB and NIV (Matthew 9:13; 12:7, quoting Hosea 6:6). The lexical meaning of the word is not really "love."

Secondly the two items are different enough to merit separate English terms.

The NEB translates the phrase in a verbal way: "faithfully keepest covenant," as does Today's English Version (TEV).

Scientific analysis of language is a fascinating and helpful discipline. When exercised in a modified way to communicate idioms that do not translate literally from one language to another, it can make a fine contribution to a basically literal translation. However, the Bible contains difficult doctrinal discussions, and there is real danger of inserting what the translator *believes* rather than what the New Testament *says*.

To demonstrate how seriously dynamic equivalence translation can undermine the Christian faith, one has only to read the TEV New Testament, which gives "death" as an equivalent of "blood" in such atonement passages as Ephesians 1:7. A death could be nonviolent, or at least not entail bloodshed. In light of the requirement for blood atonement in Leviticus, Hebrews, and also New Testament theology, such a reading seems rather undynamic and certainly is *not* equivalent!

Complete Equivalence

The term "complete equivalence" was coined by the NKJV Old Testament Editor, in discussions with the Old Testament Executive Review Committee.¹⁰

We have briefly discussed the literal method and the dynamic-equivalence method of translating. Complete equivalence is basically *the literal method* updated to include scientific insights from *linguistic analysis*. To the extent that modern usage allows, a complete-equivalence translation of such a book as the Bible will reflect as much of the original as possible.

Summarizing this method, Price writes:

> Modern research in structural linguistics has revealed the importance of syntactic structures. A great deal of the information contained in a phrase,

clause, or paragraph is encoded in its syntax. Translations that do not produce structural equivalence as well as semantic equivalence have failed to reproduce important information.[11]

Creative Connectives

A good illustration of the difference between a strictly literal rendering (here, NASB), a dynamic-equivalence translation (NIV), and a literal rendering tempered by the stylistic demands of the receptor language (NKJV), is their varied treatment of connectives, which is illustrated below.

It is well known to students of the original languages of the Scriptures that the biblical tongues are fond of short conjunctions.

In the Old Testament a very large percentage of sentences begin with the little Hebrew word *we* (or *ve* in modern Hebrew pronunciation). This is usually translated *and,* or sometimes *but* or *now* in the KJV. The result is hundreds of verses beginning with *and.*

In the New Testament there are two little words, *kai* and *de,* that connect sentences and clauses. These also are usually translated *and* in the KJV, though sometimes *also, but,* or *now.* The Evangelist Mark is so fond of the word *kai* that in the KJV you will sometimes notice several verses in a row in his Gospel that begin with *and.*

The dilemma here is that English style does not favor sentences starting with *and,* except on a limited scale. Should we make a wholesale deletion of these connectives in favor of English style and thus perhaps violate our strict view of verbal inspiration? Or should we translate nearly all of them as *and* and violate good English style?

Most modern versions, such as the NIV, choose the first option. Thousands of Hebrew *we*s, as well as Greek *kai*s and *de*s, are summarily dismissed. On the other hand, should we go the route of the KJV, ASV (1901), and NASB, and have myriads of verses starting with *and?* Or could there be a better way to translate?

There is a chart in a widely used intermediate Greek grammar[12] that highlights the fact that the little connectives *kai* and *de* can have *many* meanings depending on context. Semitic writers—and all the New Testament writers were Jewish with the probable exception of Luke—would often think Hebrew thoughts and put them in Greek words. Could the New Testament writers have felt more subtle nuances from their Hebrew roots when they wrote *kai* and *de?* Even first-year Greek students sometimes sense that one of these little words demands the translation *but* in certain contexts.

One of the tasks of our English Editor, Dr. William McDowell,[13] was to vary the English connectives in both the Old Testament and New

Testament for literary variety, but according to context. The lexicons allow many meanings. The contexts suggest several subtle nuances of thought. Why not retain as many of these connectives as English style will permit? Of course, even the 1611 KJV omits some of these little connectives, but a wholesale deletion seemed too radical to our scholars.

Working both with the Greek and Hebrew words and the demands of the context, McDowell carefully chose the *so,* the *now,* the *then*—as well as the *and* and the *but*—to begin the many sentences in both Testaments that use connectives.

The result is smoother translations, especially in the New Testament, where the Greek text often builds its argument partly by means of various logical connectives. This variety of translation is both refreshing and helpful in keeping the action moving along. Notice for example Mark 1:29-34 in the NASB, the NKJV, and the NIV. A dash means that a connective is left untranslated.

NASB	NKJV	NIV
29 And immediately after they had come out of the synagogue, they came into the house of Simon and Andrew, with James and John. 30 Now Simon's mother-in-law was lying sick with a fever; and immediately they spoke to Him about her. 31 And He came to her and raised her up, taking her by the hand, and the fever left her, and she began to wait on them. 32 And when evening had come, after the sun had set, they began bringing to Him all who were ill and those who were demon-possessed. 33 And the whole city had gathered at the door.	29 Now as soon as they had come out of the synagogue, they entered the house of Simon and Andrew, with James and John. 30 But Simon's wife's mother lay sick with a fever, and they told Him about her at once. 31 So He came and took her by the hand and lifted her up, and immediately the fever left her. And she served them. 32 [—] At evening, when the sun had set, they brought to Him all who were sick and those who were demon-possessed. 33 And the whole city was gathered together at the door.	29 [—] As soon as they left the synagogue, they went with James and John to the home of Simon and Andrew. 30 [—] Simon's mother-in-law was in bed with a fever, and they told Jesus about her. 31 So he went to her, took her hand and helped her up. The fever left her and she began to wait on them. 32 [—] That evening after sunset the people brought to Jesus all the sick and demon-pos-sessed. 33 [—] The whole town gathered at the door,

34 <u>And</u> He healed many who were ill with various diseases, and cast out many demons; and He was not permitting the demons to speak, because they knew who He was.	34 <u>Then</u> He healed many who were sick with various diseases, and cast out many demons; and He did not allow the demons to speak, because they knew Him.	34 <u>and</u> Jesus healed many who had various diseases. He also drove out many demons, but he would not let the demons speak because they knew who he was.

The NASB is to be commended for retaining all the connectives, but five out of six verses starting with *And* is poor English style. (Verses 35-44 all start with *And* as well!).

At the other extreme is the NIV, which (characteristically) deletes almost all the connectives. They are also deleted in verses 35, 36, 38, 40, 41, 42, 43, 44, and 45.

The NKJV deletes the connective in verse 32 to suggest the break in time, and translates the rest according to context. Not only is the text more complete, but it flows better, since, we believe, those little words were put in for a purpose—to connect sentences in a logical chain of thought.

Conclusion

For a standard Bible, then, we believe that a basically literal translation method, assisted by the findings of modern linguistics, will yield the optimum version.

Therefore, we respectfully request you, the reader, to examine the NKJV in the light of the guidelines and criteria we have presented. Then make your own informed decision as to whether the New King James Version is for you. We hope it is.

NOTES

[1]James D. Price, *Complete Equivalence in Bible Translation* (Nashville: Thomas Nelson Publishers, 1987), p. 5.

[2]Eugene H. Glassman, *The Translation Debate* (Downers Grove, IL: InterVarsity Press, 1981), p. 48.

[3]The Greek words are *ēsan tetagmenoi,* a periphrastic perfect passive of the verb *tassō*, "appoint," "set in order," "arrange," "constitute."

[4]Price, *Complete Equivalence,* p. 17.

[5]Glassman, *Debate,* p. 52.

[6]Ibid., pp. 56-57.

[7]A concise and fair treatment of this method is included in Price's booklet, *Complete Equivalence in Bible Translation.*

[8]Glassman, *Debate,* p. 61.

[9]This is called "hendiadys," from the Greek for "one by means of two."

[10]Dr. Price now prefers the term "Optimum Equivalence" because of the possible misreading of "complete" to mean "absolute." But see the explanations of "complete" at the beginning of this section of our book.

[11]James D. Price, unpublished monograph on Bible translating.

[12]H. E. Dana and Julius R. Mantey, *A Manual Grammar of the Greek New Testament,* (New York: The Macmillan Company, 1927), p. 257.

[13]See Appendix A for his credentials.

Conclusion

"Oh, yes sir, you should look into the New King James—they did a very thorough job of updating the text, but it still sounds like the King James. They say it's accurate and complete and I can tell that it's beautiful." We hope the saleslady in our Introduction reads this book or talks to someone who has, then revises her inadequate—not to say false—concept of what the New King James Version of the Bible is all about.

To make it easy for her we have provided a selection of informed opinion from England, Canada, and the United States who want her and others to understand the goals and achievements of the New King James Version.

I have sincerely tried to be accurate, fair, and hopefully interesting in stressing the three great qualities that our translation team worked so hard to retain from the KJV and enhance in the NKJV.

Of course I would be fooling no one if I were to pretend that I was an objective witness. First as New Testament Editor and later as Executive Editor of the New King James Version, I have put many years of my life and used much of my education in this work.

And now it's time to hear from others, a few who worked on the NKJV, and several others.

These testimonials have been chosen from a much larger selection for their variety and sincerity. I have organized them under various categories.

Children and Youth Workers

It is fitting that the first word should go to a lady, Mrs. Dan Mosher, since she is not only a Sunday school teacher and home schooler, but also was my secretary in the first few years of the NKJV project. She typed the New Testament from scratch—and retyped—and retyped, as well as making valuable contributions on current usage and style.

A Sunday School Teacher

The New King James translation has been a great help to me in teaching children's Sunday school classes and Bible clubs. Not having to explain archaic words or word order in Scripture passages and memory verses saves valuable teaching time. This is important when you're dealing with the limited attention span of children! They are able to learn and recite verses with more understanding.

At the same time, the traditional rhythm and outstanding English style of the older King James Version is preserved, enabling children to experience God's Word as great literature as they learn its spiritual truths in a language they can easily understand.

Frances Mosher
Sunday School Teacher
Christ Congregation
Dallas, Texas

A Youth Leader

For the past forty years, the Awana ministry has been building lives on the Word of God. As Awana shares in the spiritual training of young people around the world, we recognize the importance of a clear presentation of the Scriptures. After much prayerful consideration, we decided to use the New King James Version in the Awana publications. We believe that incorporating the NKJV into the Awana materials will help young people to better understand God's Word.

Dr. Art Rorheim
President
AWANA Clubs International
Streamwood, Illinois

A CEF Leader

Is there anything more important than sharing God's Word with the youngest and ripest mission fields in language they can understand? Recently Child Evangelism Fellowship has chosen to print our Visualized Bible Verses in The New King James Version for easier comprehension. We use visuals, sign language, music, and games to teach, repeat, and review these verses. But the most important tool for a boy or girl to associate with the memory verses is his or her own copy of God's Word. If a child comes to a Good News Club or summer Five-Day Club and has no Bible, he is given one after coming three times. I have observed with joy the illumination of the Holy Spirit as a child sees that the copy of God's precious Word in his hands matches what the teacher has on the large visual.

Susan Pearl Tyler
Supervisor of Teacher Training
Child Evangelism Fellowship
Dallas, Texas

A Campus Evangelical Leader

I'm really delighted with the New King James Version. Now we have a Bible that is easily memorized as well as being easily understood.

Bill Bright
President
Campus Crusade for Christ
San Bernardino, California

An Evangelist and Youth Leader

I have devoted my life to counseling young people, teaching them the moral precepts of Christian living. Because of this, I favor words and language that youth can understand. The New King James Version fulfills an important need for a contemporary version with sound doctrine kept intact. So many times translators have a tendency to sacrifice traditional biblical theology in order to keep the text "modern" for today's readers. The New King James Version does an excellent job of retaining the great truth of the Bible, at the same time removing the confusing archaisms.

Jack Wyrtzen
Word of Life Fellowship
Schroon Lake, New York

Educators

Those who teach the Bible on a college or Seminary level want a version that is readable yet reliably close to the original. The following educators believe that the NKJV meets those needs.

A Seminary Professor

The NKJV is the only modern translation that does not either call into question or omit all or parts of scores of New Testament verses. Yet it provides the fullest set of footnotes dealing with textual matters to be found outside of a Greek New Testament itself.

For example, Mark 9:44 and 46 do not exist in the NIV, RSV, NASB, TEV, and NEB. But the overwhelming evidence based on antiquity, catholicity, continuity, and number is clearly in favor of the authenticity of those verses. Similarly, the familiar fifty-eight-word (KJV) Lord's Prayer in Luke 11:2—4 is reduced to only thirty-seven words in the RSV and NASB, and shrinks to only thirty-four words in the NIV. The NKJV has fifty-nine words.

Dr. James Borland
Professor of Bible and Theology
Liberty University
Lynchburg, Virginia

A Canadian Scholar

Of all the modern translations, my favorite is the New King James Version. This revision was born out of a desire to maintain the literary and spiritual traditions of a familiar version, and involved the work of evangelical scholars who updated the grammar and syntax as well as modernizing obsolete expressions. The revision was governed by the principle of "complete equivalence," which involved a measured rendering of each word and phrase so that accuracy in translation rather than paraphrase was the dominant consideration.

Dr. R. K. Harrison
Emeritus Professor of Old Testament
Wycliffe College
University of Toronto
Toronto, Canada

A Chairman of the Board

I have observed that preachers who use modern translations and paraphrases seldom quote the Word enough. Most modern versions are too wordy and not easy to quote. The New King James, like the old King James (which I've read fifty-four times), is very quotable. I have recommended the NKJV to our faculty, staff, and students. It is now my favorite version.

Mrs. Freda T. Lindsay
Chairman of the Board
Christ for the Nations
Dallas, Texas

A Greek Scholar

The New King James Bible has several excellencies which commend it, three of which are its English, its philosophy of translation, and its basic text. . . . As for translation philosophy, the New King James aims at faithfulness in the rendering of the original languages. It avoids stiff literalness on the one hand and interpretive paraphrase on the other. It seeks to present what the inspired writer says without trying to explain what he means. This is what most of us want, is it not? We want to know what God says, not what some translator thinks He meant.

†**Dr. Harry Sturz**
Professor Emeritus of Greek
Biola University
La Mirada, California

A Lutheran Professor

I heartily recommend for serious consideration the use of the NKJV as the *standard English translation* for the following reasons: its literary quality, its ease in memorization, and its accuracy in following the Greek text faithfully.

Dr. Robert Hoerber
Professor of Exegetical Theology
Concordia Seminary
St. Louis, Missouri

An NIV Scholar

The New King James Version should find its most ready acceptance among those who treasure the Authorized Version for reasons of lifelong familiarity and confidence in the traditional. In particular, the eminently memorizable character of the Authorized Version is carried over in the New King James Version. Also, that song-like cadence, which so naturally impresses the phrasing on the memory of the reader, is the same quality that enhances the essential vitality of private and public worship. Along with fidelity of translation, these inherent qualities of the Word of God must be preserved by the church.

The New International Version is an entirely new translation written in the language of the twentieth century.

The New King James Version is a very careful revision of the King James Version. It is more accurate, because it is rendered in the manner in which things were said in the original language. The Bible is a covenant document from God addressed to His people. We have a responsibility to present God's Word in as faithful a rendition as possible.

Milton C. Fisher
Professor of Old Testament
Theological Seminary of the
Reformed Episcopal Church
Philadelphia, Pennsylvania

Evangelists and Missionaries

Children and youth work, as well as teaching generally, include an evangelistic outreach. But there are those—called evangelists and missionaries—whose main mission in life is to reach the non-Christian and unchurched world. These people, too, are being helped by the clarity of the NKJV.

A Young Evangelist

The first real book I ever read at seven and eight years of age was the King James Version of the Bible. Yes, even Leviticus and Numbers! The King James was the version I used to memorize my first Bible verses, play my first "sword drills" in Vacation Bible School, and preach my first sermon.

For me, the King James Bible is more than a translation—it's part of my thoughts, prayers, and vocabulary. As a writer, King James phrases glide from my pen. As a preacher, King James cadences flow through my sermons. As an evangelist, I can't imagine quoting the most famous verse in the Bible, John 3:16, without saying it like the King James said it.

Having said all this, however, why do I like the *New* King James? Because it's all the things the old King James was, only better. It's much easier to read. It's clearer when you're interpreting a passage. And it's a great aid in communication.

Whether I'm studying for a sermon, witnessing to a person in need of Christ, or reading my daily devotions, I feel right at home with the New King James. It's a faithful old friend and an outstanding new friend combined in one.

God has blessed His English-speaking church in the world today with this brilliant translation of His holy, inerrant Word, a translation that continues a four-hundred-year-old tradition of beauty and reliability, and yet pioneers fresh, conservative ground for a new generation.

Do I use the old King James anymore? No. Why should I, when I have the New King James—everything that was great in the old, plus a whole lot more? And just in case you have any doubt, I *love* the New King James!

Frank D. Carmical
Evangelist
Plano Bible Chapel
Plano, Texas

A Television Evangelist

The New King James Version makes reading the Bible much clearer but in no way dilutes the truth or distracts from the most effective flow found in the original King James.

James Robison
Evangelist
Euless, Texas

A Former Missionary

As one who has long appreciated the worshipful quality of the King James Bible, I have recently turned to the New King James as my primary source of spiritual instruction and inspiration. I believe this change is explained on three accounts: first, the similarity of the newer edition to the older one in which I received my early and later spiritual training; second, the elimination of archaic English greatly eases my reading; and third, my enjoyment of biblical *poetry* as poetry, since these passages have been cast in beautiful poetic form.

The New King James revisers have accomplished an amazing task of retaining the accuracy and majesty that are unique in the King James Bible, while at the same time vastly improving its communication qualities.

Jean Anthony McDowell
Former Missionary
Curriculum Research Specialist
Orlando, Florida

Pastors and Church Leaders

Probably the most important users of the Bible are those who preach from it every week from pulpits all over the world. While some ministers use the Bible sparingly in their preaching, those who believe in expounding the whole counsel of God, such as those quoted below, desire a very accurate yet worshipful translation for public reading and exposition.

A Former President of the Southern Baptist Convention

Understanding will be improved by a clearer rendering where language has changed through the years. There is no translation on earth that has the beauty of the New King James Bible.

Dr. Adrian Rogers
Pastor
Bellevue Baptist Church
Memphis, Tennessee

A California Pastor

In January, 1984, we announced that we would be reading publicly from the NKJV each Sunday and would be preaching and teaching from that translation from then on. It has become exciting to hear the unified reading of the Scriptures each week. For those who have been enamored by the King James Bible, it has not been difficult for them to switch. I can certainly recommend this approach to any congregation which sees the value of public reading of God's Word as well as the private study thereof. This unified approach has enhanced our spiritual life and our coming together in the unity of Christ.

Glen D. Cole
Pastor
Capital Christian Center
Sacramento, California

An English Minister

We surely want a Bible that is both accurate and readable. The issue at stake cannot be regarded lightly. Let me sincerely and earnestly commend to you the New King James Version. . . . I am profoundly thankful to God that we have at last a "trusted text that is easy to read" and is available from your local Christian bookshop.

Rev. David Fountain
Pastor
Spring Road Evangelical Church
Sholing, Southampton, England

A National Baptist Convention Pastor

I particularly like its clarity and its reverent phrases and sentences. It is a book that young people can understand and identify with.

Dr. John W. Williams
Pastor
St. Stephen Baptist Church
Kansas City, Missouri

A Pentecostal Pastor

As a Sunday school teacher for about twenty years and as a pastor for another ten, I have done a lot of reading in and studying from Bibles. I expect I've read more than ten different translations completely through, some of them several times. . . .

After all that reading and studying, I sincerely believe the New King James Version to be the best of the lot for most practical purposes. It parallels the King James Version closely enough for ease in using the study aids keyed to that version. It retains enough of the style of the KJV to make it familiar to old timers like me, and it does away with the archaic wording which makes the KJV difficult to read aloud and be understood by new readers.

David E. Beneze
Pastor
International Church of the Four-Square Gospel
Colorado Springs, Colorado

A Presbyterian Minister

The original authors of the King James Version of the Bible reached a pinnacle of excellence in the use of the English language which has, in my opinion, never been equalled or excelled. Therefore, the Bible holds a unique place in the hearts of millions of people. The New King James Version will thus retain the beauty of the original while removing its few blemishes.

Dr. D. James Kennedy
Pastor
Coral Ridge Presbyterian Church
Ft. Lauderdale, Florida

A Southern Baptist Pastor

I highly recommend the NKJV. I firmly believe that it is the very best version of God's Word in English. . . . This version is translated *completely* in current English. It is delightful to read; however, accuracy is not sacrificed for readability. This rendering of God's Word is true to the Greek, Hebrew, and Aramaic.

The New King James Version is based on the same families of manuscripts as that of the traditional KJV. Modern readers who have been accustomed to the KJV are not stumped by the reverse order of certain verses that marks other modern versions. Familiar passages are not omitted in the NKJV.

The NKJV is quite honest. In the study editions, elaborate references to variant readings in families of manuscripts are included.

Dr. Lawrence Dee Burks
Pastor
First Baptist Church
Goodlettsville, Tennessee

A Bible Church Pastor

God wants you to understand His Word so that you can obey Him. It is as we are "filled with the knowledge of His will in all wisdom and spiritual understanding" that we will be able to "walk worthy of the Lord, fully pleasing Him, being fruitful in every good work and increasing in the knowledge of God" (Colossians 1:9, 10). God desires that we be transformed by the renewing of our mind as we are exposed to His Word (compare Romans 12:2).

The problem is we tend to hold on to tradition. That's fine until it interferes with understanding and obeying God's Word. The story is told of a man who began walking through a secluded portion of a Russian imperial garden. When he was stopped by an armed soldier, he identified himself and asked what the soldier was guarding. The guard replied, "I don't know. The captain ordered me and three other men to stand guard here and we've been taking turns for years now." Out of curiosity, the man called the captain of the guard and inquired of him why there was a guard in that part of the garden. He didn't know either, except that palace regulations called for it.

The man began to investigate. He discovered that four men had been assigned to guard that post for the past 125 years. A search of the archives uncovered the source of the regulation. Catherine the Great had once planted a rose bush at the spot and had ordered the palace guard to see to it that the shrub was not trampled down. Soldiers were posted to watch the bush! For the next 125 years, soldiers stood guard. No one ever asked, "Is this a standing order or is it simply tradition?"

Are we bound to the King James Version of the Bible because of tradition, or is it the desire of our hearts to get the most accurate translation of the Word of God possible so that we can understand it and do what God has said? The translators of the original Authorized Version of the Bible said that their purpose was not to "make a new translation . . . but to make a good one better." That is precisely what the translators of the New King James have done. Do we want a better translation or do we merely want to hold on to tradition?

Dr. Michael Cocoris
Senior Pastor
Church of the Open Door
Glendora, California

After reading all these testimonies all I can do is to quote the words that Augustine heard in his garden so long ago that led to his conversion to Christ: *"Tolle, lege"* — "Take up and read!"

Appendix A

The NKJV Teams

To fulfill the purpose of the New King James Version of the Bible, over 130 scholars, editors, church leaders, and Christian laity were commissioned to work on the project.

To maintain a singleness of purpose, each person was commissioned only after pledging commitment to the basic aims of the project. All signed a statement of faith declaring belief that the Scriptures in their entirety are the uniquely inspired Word of God, free from error in their original autographs.

NKJV Translators - Old Testament

The following scholars individually revised one or more books of the Old Testament. The schools and positions are those of the period when the NKJV was being produced.

Names marked with a cross are now deceased.

Dr. Ronald B. Allen, B.A., Th.M., Th.D.
Professor, Old Testament Language and Exegesis
Western Conservative Baptist Seminary
Portland, Oregon

Dr. Barry J. Beitzel, B.A., M.A., Ph.D.
Associate Professor of Old Testament and Semitic Languages
Trinity Evangelical Divinity School
Deerfield, Illinois

Dr. Walter R. Bodine, B.A., Th.M., Ph.D.
Associate Professor of Semitic Languages and Old Testament
Dallas Theological Seminary
Dallas, Texas

Dr. Newton L. Bush, B.S., Th.M., Th.D.
Editor, Minister
Bethel Christian Union Chapel
Elida, Ohio

Dr. E. Clark Copeland, B.A., S.T.M., D.D., Th.D.
Professor of Old Testament
Reformed Presbyterian Theological Seminary
Pittsburgh, Pennsylvania

Dr. Leonard J. Coppes, B.A., B.D., Th.M., Th.D.
Minister
Calvary Orthodox Presbyterian Church
Harrisville, Pennsylvania

Dr. Arthur L. Farstad, B.A., Th.M., Th.D.
Executive Editor of the NKJV
Dallas, Texas

Dr. Harvey E. Finley, A.B., B.D., Ph.D.
Professor of Old Testament
Nazarene Theological Seminary
Kansas City, Missouri

Dr. D. David Garland, B.A., B.D., Th.D.
Professor of Old Testament and Hebrew
Southwestern Baptist Theological Seminary
Fort Worth, Texas

Dr. Paul R. Gilchrist, B.A., B.D., Ph.D.
Professor of Biblical Studies
Covenant College
Lookout Mountain, Tennessee

Dr. Louis Goldberg, B.S., M.A., B.D., Th.M., Th.D.
Professor of Theology and Jewish Studies
Moody Bible Institute
Chicago, Illinois

Rev. Geoffrey Watts Grogan, B.D., M.Th.
Principal
Bible Training Insitute
Glasgow, Scotland

Dr. Victor Paul Hamilton, B.A., M.A., B.D., Th.M., Ph.D.
Associate Professor of Religion
Asbury College
Wilmore, Kentucky

Dr. Allan M. Harman, B.A., M. Litt., B.D., Th.M., Th.D.
Professor of Old Testament
Reformed Theological College
Victoria, Australia

Dr. Edward E. Hindson, B.A., M.A., Th.M., Th.D.
Professor of Religion
Liberty Baptist College (now University)
Lynchburg, Virginia

Dr. Horace D. Hummel, B.A., B.D., S.T.M., Ph.D.
Associate Professor of Old Testament
Concordia Seminary
St. Louis, Missouri

Dr. David K. Huttar, B.A., M.A., Ph.D.
Professor of Old Testament and Greek
Nyack College
Nyack, New York

Dr. Meredith G. Kline, A.B., Th.B., Th.M., Ph.D.
Professor of Old Testament
Gordon-Conwell Theological Seminary
South Hamilton, Massachusetts

Dr. Donald A. Leggett, B.A., B.D., Th.M., Th.D.
Professor of Old Testament
Ontario Theological Seminary
Willowdale, Ontario, Canada

Dr. Allan A. MacRae, B.A., M.A., Th.B., M.A., Ph.D.
President, Professor of Old Testament
Biblical School of Theology
Hatfield, Pennsylvania

Dr. Elmer A. Martens, B.A., B.Ed., B.D., Ph.D.
President, Professor of Old Testament
Mennonite Brethren Biblical Seminary
Fresno, California

Dr. William H. McDowell, B.A., M. Div., M.C.S., Litt. D.
Professor of Philosophy and Religion
Florida Southern College
Orlando, Florida

Dr. Eugene H. Merrill, B.A., M.A., Ph.D.
Associate Professor of Semitics and Old Testament Studies
Dallas Theological Seminary
Dallas, Texas

Dr. Gerald I. Miller, B.A., M. Div., Ph.D.
Chairman, Division of Foreign Language
Asbury College
Wilmore, Kentucky

Dr. Richard O. Rigsby, B.A., M. Div., Th.D.
Associate Professor of Semitic Languages and Old Testament
Talbot Theological Seminary
La Mirada, California

Dr. Allen P. Ross, B.A., Th.M., Th.D., Ph.D.
Professor of Old Testament
Dallas Theological Seminary
Dallas, Texas

Dr. Glenn E. Schaefer, B.S., B.D., Th.M., Ph.D.
Chairman, Department of Bible, Theology, and Mission
Simpson College
San Francisco, California

Dr. Gary V. Smith, B.A., M.A., Ph.D.
Dean, Chairman, Department of Old Testament
Winnipeg Theological Seminary
Otterburne, Manitoba, Canada

Rev. Arthur Steltzer, B.A., B.D., Th.M.
Pastor/Teacher
Emmanuel Orthodox Presbyterian Church
Wilmington, Delaware

Dr. William White, Jr., B.S., M.Div., Th.M., Ph.D.
Writer, Editor
Warrington, Pennsylvania

Dr. Willem A. VanGemeren, B.A., B.D., M.A., Ph.D.
Professor of Old Testament
Reformed Theological Seminary
Jackson, Mississippi

NKJV Translators—New Testament

The following scholars individually revised one or more books of the New Testament.

The schools and positions are those of the period when the NKJV was being produced.

Names marked with a cross are now deceased.

†Dr. Boyce W. Blackwelder, A.B., B.D., A.M., Th.D.
Anderson College
Anderson, Indiana

†Dr. E. M. Blaiklock, O.B.E., Litt.D.
Professor Emeritus of Classics
University of Auckland
Titirangi, Auckland, New Zealand

Dr. James L. Boyer, B.A., B.D., S.T.M., Th.D.
Professor Emeritus of New Testament and Greek
Grace Theological Seminary
Winona Lake, Indiana

Dr. John A. Burns, B.A., Cert. Supérieur, Th.M., Th.D.
Chairman, New Testament Department
Liberty Baptist Seminary
Lynchburg, Virginia

Mr. William J. Cameron, M.A., B.D.
Principal Emeritus
Free Church of Scotland College
Edinburgh, Scotland

Dr. A. Glenn Campbell, B.A., Th.M., Th.D.
Professor Emeritus of New Testament, Greek, and Theology
Montana Institute of the Bible
Ottawa, Kansas

Dr. Gary G. Cohen, B.S., M.Div.
S.T.M., Th.D.
Lecturer
Miami Christian College
Miami, Florida

†Dr. Huber L. Drumwright,
B.A., B.D., Th.D.
Dean, School of Theology
Southwestern Baptist Theological
Seminary
Fort Worth, Texas

Dr. William R. Eichhorst, B.A.,
Th.M., Th.D.
President of Academic Affairs
Winnipeg Bible College and
Theological Seminary
Otterburne, Manitoba, Canada

Dr. Arthur L. Farstad, B.A.,
Th.M., Th.D.
New Testament and Executive
Editor
Dallas, Texas

Dr. Lewis A. Foster, A.B., M.A.,
M.Div., B.D., S.T.M., Ph.D.
Professor of New Testament
Cincinnati Seminary
Cincinnati, Ohio

Dr. Virtus E. Gideon, B.A., B.D.,
Ph.D.
Professor of New Testament and
Greek
Southwestern Baptist Theological
Seminary
Fort Worth, Texas

Dr. Robert L. Hendren, B.A.,
M.A., Ph.D.
Minister
Donelson Church of Christ
Nashville, Tennessee

Dr. Robert G. Hoerber, A.A., A.B.,
M.A., Ph.D.
Professor of Exegetical Theology
Concordia Seminary
St. Louis, Missouri

Dr. Ronald H. Jones, Th. Dip.,
M. Div., Ph.D.
Associate Professor
Victory Tabernacle Baptist Church
Norfolk, Virginia

Dr. Charles R. Smith, B.A., Th.M.,
Th.D.
Professor of Christian Theology and
Greek
Grace Theological Seminary
Winona Lake, Indiana

Dr. John A. Sproule, B.S., Th.M.,
Th.D.
Associate Professor of New Testament
and Greek
Grace Theological Seminary
Winona Lake, Indiana

†Dr. Harry A. Sturz, B.A., B.D.,
Th.M., Th.D.
Professor of Greek
Biola College
La Mirada, California

Dr. Joseph S. Wang, B.S., B.D., Th.M., Ph.D.
Professor of New Testament
Asbury Theological Seminary
Wilmore, Kentucky

Dr. A. Skevington Wood, B.A., Ph.D.
Principal
Cliff College
Calver, Sheffield, England

Dr. Phillip R. Williams, B.A., Th.B., Th.M., Ph.D.
Registrar, Professor of New Testament
Northwest Baptist Seminary
Tacoma, Washington

Consultants

Besides the translators, several consultants were called in on various problems. Prof. Hodges also did translation work at a later stage.

Dr. Charles F. Aling, A.B., M.A., Ph.D.
Professor of Archaeology
Temple Baptist Theological Seminary

Mrs. Winifred Griffith Thomas Gillespie
Book Editor

Mr. Edward C. Hepworth, B.S., M.Div.
Bible Editor

Prof. Zane C. Hodges, A.B., Th.M.
Professor of New Testament Literature and Exegesis
Dallas Theological Seminary

Prof. Robert V. McCabe, A.B., M.Div., Th.M.
Professor of Biblical Studies
Tennessee Temple University

Dr. Herbert M. McCollum, D.V.M.
Biological Consultant

Dr. Steven R. Schrader, B.S., M.Div., Th.M., Th.D.
Assistant Professor of Old Testament and Homiletics
Liberty University

Prof. Richard D. Sorrells, B.S., M.S., M.Div.
Professor of Christian Education and Greek
Tennessee Temple University

Appendix B

The NKJV Editors

The initial editing was done by the translators themselves. Each book was carefully scrutinized by other translators who had done books of comparable size. For example, Dr. Philip Williams, who revised 2 Corinthians, also interacted with Dr. Sturz' revision of Hebrews, and vice versa.

Following detailed guidelines drawn up by the editors, translators and several members of the Overview Committees, the English Editor, Dr. William McDowell, in collaboration with the Old Testament Editor, Dr. James D. Price, and the New Testament Editor (later Executive Editor of the NKJV), Dr. Arthur L. Farstad, carefully reviewed every word of the entire Bible. Meanwhile, many members of the Overview Committees were constantly contributing their reactions, suggestions, and criticisms to the book or books that they chose to work with.

The Executive Review Committees

After the text of both Testaments was well advanced, President Sam Moore of Thomas Nelson Publishers established Executive Review Committees for both Testaments.

The New Testament Executive Review Committee

Since the New Testament is much shorter than the Old, and was finished first, Dr. Farstad, who was originally New Testament Editor, was asked to join the Old Testament ERC when the New Testament was nearly finished. He was then made Executive Editor of the NKJV.

All of the following members of the ERC read through the typescripts of the entire New Testament, and made written suggestions. These were taken up and acted upon by the assembled ERC. These meetings met for a week or two at a time in various parts of the U.S.A., Canada, and finally, Scotland.

Chairman
Dr. Arthur L. Farstad, B.A., Th.M., Th.D.
New Testament and Executive Editor
Dallas, Texas

Dr. William H. McDowell, B.A., M.Div., M.C.S., Litt.D.
Professor of Philosophy and Religion
Florida Southern College
Orlando, Florida

Dr. Robert L. Reymond, B.A., M.A., Ph.D.
Professor of Systematic Theology and Apologetics
Covenant Theological Seminary
St. Louis, Missouri

Dr. Robert L. Hughes, B.A., M.Div., Th.D.
President
Pensacola Baptist Seminary
Pensacola, Florida

†Dr. Harry A. Sturz, B.A., B.D., Th.M., Th.D.
Professor Emeritus of Greek
Biola College
La Mirada, California

Dr. Alfred Martin, A.B., Th.M., Th.D.
Professor of Bible
Dallas Bible College
Dallas, Texas

Dr. William Curtis Vaughan, A.B., B.D., Th.D.
Professor of New Testament
Southwestern Baptist Theological Seminary
Fort Worth, Texas

The Old Testament Executive Review Committee

All of the following members of the ERC read through the typescripts of the entire Old Testament, and made written suggestions. These were taken up and acted upon by the assembled ERC. These meetings met for a week or two at a time in various parts of the U.S.A., Canada, and finally, Scotland.

Chairman
Dr. James D. Price, B.S., M.Div., Ph.D.
Professor, Department of Old Testament
Temple Baptist Theological Seminary
Chattanooga, Tennessee

Dr. William H. McDowell, B.A., M.Div., M.C.S., Litt.D.
Professor of Philosophy and Religion
Florida Southern College
Orlando, Florida

Dr. Arthur L. Farstad, B.A., Th.M., Th.D.
New Testament and Executive Editor
Dallas, Texas

Dr. D. David Garland, B.A., B.D., Th.D.
Professor of Old Testament
Southwestern Baptist Theological
Seminary
Fort Worth, Texas

Dr. Paul R. Gilchrist, B.A., B.D., Ph.D.
Professor of Biblical Studies
Covenant College
Lookout Mountain, Tennessee

Dr. R. K. Harrison, B.D., M.Th., Ph.D.
Professor of Old Testament
Wycliffe College
Toronto, Ontario, Canada

Dr. G. Herbert Livingston, A.B., B.D., Ph.D.
Professor of Old Testament
Chairman of the Division of Biblical
Studies
Asbury Theological Seminary
Wilmore, Kentucky

Appendix C

Commonwealth Oversight Committee

Originally founded in Great Britain (Edinburgh, 1798), Thomas Nelson Publishers has never forgotten its British roots. Nelson did not want this to be merely an "American Version," but like the KJV, one for the whole English-speaking church. For this reason scholars were chosen from England, Scotland, Canada, Australia, New Zealand, as well as from the U.S.A. One scholar from Europe (Netherlands) and one from Asia (Taiwan) very appropriately represented the millions who use English beyond the English-speaking countries as such.

An attempt was made to avoid expressions that are current in only one part of the English-speaking community. However, since there are certain expressions and spelling differences that do occur in British and American English, the NKJV is available in both Commonwealth and American editions. The British usage edition is distributed by The Bible Societies.

The following participated in the initial meeting in London in early 1976. Several also attended the final meetings at St. Andrews University in July of 1981 and contributed their wisdom in written form at other times:

Sir Cyril Black
Justice of the Peace,
Deputy Lieutenant
Beaumont House
London, England

Rev. Raymond Brown
Principal
Spurgeon College
London, England

Rev. David B. Bubbers
General Secretary
Church Pastoral Aid Society
London, England

Mr. Donald J. Crowther
Numismatic Consultant
Sevenoaks, Kent, England

Mr. Edward England
Edward England Books Ltd.
East Sussex, England

†Dr. James William Fairbairn
University of London
London, England

Rt. Rev. A. W. Goodwin-Hudson
Bishop
Newton Solney, Derbyshire,
England

Mr. David R. L. Porter
Writer, Editor
Greatham, Hampshire, England

Sir J. Eric Richardson
Director
London Polytechnic
London, England

Rev. David H. Wheaton
Principal
Oakhill Anglican Theological College
London, England

Rt. Rev. Maurice A. P. Wood
Bishop
Chaplain to Her Majesty the Queen
Norwich, England

North American Overview Committee

Two large meetings of the North American Overview Committee met at Nashville and Chicago in 1975 to assist in preparing guidelines for the NKJV. Nearly all felt that the project was worthy of the time, money, and effort that would be invested. Members of this committee included:

Dr. Porter L. Barrington
Evangelist, Author
World Witness Evangelism
Thousand Oaks, California

†Dr. Batsell Barrett Baxter
Chairman, Department of Bible
David Lipscomb College
Nashville, Tennessee

Dr. B. Clayton Bell
Senior Minister
Highland Park Presbyterian Church
Dallas, Texas

Rev. D. Stuart Briscoe
Senior Pastor
Elmbrook Church
Waukesha, Wisconsin

Dr. Kenneth L. Chafin
Pastor
South Main Baptist Church
Houston, Texas

Dr. J. Richard Chase
President
Wheaton College
Wheaton, Illinois

Dr. Robert Coleman
Professor of Evangelism
Asbury Theological Seminary
Wilmore, Kentucky

Dr. Cortez Cooper
Senior Pastor
Christ Presbyterian Church
Nashville, Tennessee

Dr. W. A. Criswell
Senior Pastor
First Baptist Church
Dallas, Texas

†Mrs. Mary C. Crowley
Founder, President
Home Interiors & Gifts, Inc.
Dallas, Texas

Mrs. Millie Dienert
World Prayer Fellowship
Philadelphia, Pennsylvania

Rev. Truman E. Dollar
Pastor
Kansas City Baptist Temple
Kansas City, Missouri

Dr. Leo Eddleman
Old Testament Semitic Languages
Criswell Center for Biblical Studies
Dallas, Texas

Dr. Jerry Falwell
Evangelist, Pastor
Thomas Road Baptist Church
Lynchburg, Virginia

V. Rev. Peter E. Gillquist
Author, Lecturer, Priest
Isla Vista, California

Rev. William S. Glass
President
Bill Glass Evangelistic Association
Dallas, Texas

Dr. Ben Haden
Radio and TV Speaker, Pastor
First Presbyterian Church
Chattanooga, Tennessee

Dr. Richard Halverson
Chaplain
United States Senate
Washington, D.C.

Rev. Marlin C. Hardman
Pastor
Covenant Community Church
Falls Church, Virginia

Dr. A. V. Henderson
Pastor
Temple Baptist Church
Detroit, Michigan

Dr. Howard G. Hendricks
Chairman, Department of Christian
Education
Dallas Theological Seminary
Dallas, Texas

Dr. E. V. Hill
Senior Pastor
Mt. Zion Baptist Church
Los Angeles, California

Dr. Herschel H. Hobbs
Pastor Emeritus
Southern Baptist Convention
Oklahoma City, Oklahoma

Mr. David L. Hofer
President, Manager
National Religious Broadcasters
Dinuba, California

Dr. Donald E. Hoke
Senior Pastor
Cedar Springs Presbyterian Church
Knoxville, Tennessee

Dr. Warren C. Hultgren
Senior Minister
First Baptist Church
Tulsa, Oklahoma

Dr. John J. Hurt, Jr.
Editor Emeritus
Baptist Standard
Dallas, Texas

Dr. Curtis Hutson
President, *Sword of the Lord*
Murfreesboro, Tennessee

Dr. James T. Jeremiah
Chancellor
Cedarville College
Cedarville, Ohio

Dr. L. C. Johnson
President Emeritus
Free Will Baptist Bible College
Nashville, Tennessee

Dr. Rufus Jones
Editor
International Literature Foundation
Wheaton, Illinois

Dr. D. James Kennedy
Senior Minister
Coral Ridge Presbyterian Church
Fort Lauderdale, Florida

Dr. Jay Kesler
President
Youth for Christ, Inc., U.S.A.
Wheaton, Illinois

Rev. Charles W. Keysor
Associate Professor in Christian
Journalism
Asbury College
Wilmore, Kentucky

Dr. Tim F. LaHaye
President, Family Life Seminars
El Cajon, California

Dr. Harold Lindsell
Editor Emeritus
Christianity Today
Laguna Hills, California

Rev. Craig Massey
Author, Lecturer
Des Plaines, Illinois

Dr. Duke K. McCall
President
Sothern Baptist Theological Seminary
Louisville, Kentucky

Dr. David L. McKenna
President
Asbury Theological Seminary
Wilmore, Kentucky

Dr. J. Robertson McQuilken
President
Columbia Bible College
Columbia, South Carolina

Mr. Donald R. Meredith
President
Christian Family Life
Little Rock, Arkansas

Dr. Jess C. Moody
Senior Pastor
First Baptist Church
Van Nuys, California

Dr. W. Stanley Mooneyham
President
World Vision International
Monrovia, California

Dr. Henry Morris
Director, Institute for Creation Research
El Cajon, California

Dr. Clyde M. Narramore
President, Director
Narramore Christian Foundation
Rosemead, California

†Dr. Harold J. Ockenga
President Emeritus
Gordon-Conwell Theological Seminary
South Hamilton, Massachusetts

Dr. Lloyd John Ogilvie
Senior Pastor
First Presbyterian Church
Hollywood, California

Rev. Luis Palau
Founder
Luis Palau Evangelistic Association
Portland, Oregon

Dr. Donald B. Patterson
Senior Minister
First Presbyterian Church
Jackson, Mississippi

Dr. J. Dwight Pentecost
Professor of Bible Exposition
Dallas Theological Seminary
Dallas, Texas

Dr. Robert E. Picirilli
Academic Dean
Free Will Baptist Bible College
Nashville, Tennessee

Mr. Matthew S. Prince
President, New Life, Inc.
Knoxville, Tennessee

Dr. Earl D. Radmacher
President, Professor of Systematic Theology
Western Conservative Baptist Seminary
Portland, Oregon

Dr. Walter R. Roehrs
Professor Emeritus of Old Testament
Concordia Seminary
St. Louis, Missouri

Dr. Adrian P. Rogers
Senior Pastor
Bellevue Baptist Church
Memphis, Tennessee

†Dr. Harlin J. Roper
President, Evangelical Projects
Dallas, Texas

Dr. Samuel Schultz
Professor Emeritus, Wheaton College
Board of Trustees, Gordon-Conwell Theological Seminary
Lexington, Massachusetts

†**Dr. Richard H. Seume**
Chaplain, Dallas Theological Seminary
Dallas, Texas

Rev. Jack B. Taylor
President
Dimensions in Christian Living
Fort Worth, Texas

Dr. Arthur Joseph Temple
Pastor, Abilene Bible Church
Abilene, Texas

Dr. Howard (Tim) Timmons
Director, Seminarist
Maximum Life Communications
Corona del Mar, California

Dr. Elmer Towns
Dean, Professor of Systematic Theology
Liberty Baptist Seminary
Lynchburg, Virginia

Rev. Nathaniel A. Urshan
General Superintendent
United Pentecostal Church
Hazelwood, Missouri

Dr. Abe C. Van Der Puy
Chairman of the Board, World Radio Missionary Fellowship, Inc.
Opa Locka, Florida

Dr. John Wesley White
The Billy Graham Evangelistic Association
Willowdale, Ontario, Canada

Rev. Bruce H. Wilkinson
President, Walk Through the Bible Ministries, Inc.
Smyrna, Georgia

Dr. John W. Williams
Pastor
St. Stephen Baptist Church
Kansas City, Missouri

Dr. Thomas F. Zimmerman
General Superintendent
The General Council of the Assemblies of God
Springfield, Missouri

Appendix D

The Nashville Convocation

The Nashville Convocation of August 13th and 14th, 1984, consisted of two groups.

The larger group was composed of distinguished Christian leaders whose counsel was sought on proposed finishing touches to the New King James Version after it had been in print for two years.

Most of the smaller group, the translators, had already been active in the production of the NKJV, but two eminent New Testament scholars, Dr. Borland and Professor Hodges were invited to join this select group.

New King James Bible Review Committee

Dr. Paul Alford
President
Toccoa Falls College

Dr. Bill Bright
President
Campus Crusade for Christ International

Mrs. Jill Briscoe
Author, Lecturer

Rev. Joseph Brown
Director, Speaker
Grace Memorial Hour

Dr. Harold Buls
Professor of Exegetical Theology
Concordia Theological Seminary

*Dr. Richard Chase
President
Wheaton College

Mrs. Evelyn Christenson
Chairperson
United Prayer Ministries

*Dr. Robert Coleman
Chairman
School of World Mission and Evangelism
Trinity Evangelical Divinity School

Dr. Billie Friel
Pastor
First Baptist Church
Mt. Juliet, Tennessee

Mr. Alan George
President
Child Evangelism Fellowship

*Ben Haden
Pastor, Speaker
First Presbyterian Church
Chattanooga, Tennessee

Dr. Jack Hayford
Senior Pastor
The Church on the Way
Van Nuys, California

*Dr. E. V. Hill
Senior Pastor
Mt. Zion Baptist Church
Los Angeles, California

*Dr. Herschel H. Hobbs
Pastor Emeritus
First Baptist Church
Oklahoma City, Oklahoma

Dr. Peter Kreeft
Professor of Philosophy
Boston College

Dr. Billy Melvin
Executive Director
National Association of
Evangelicals

Dr. Stephen Olford
President
Encounter Ministries, Inc.

*Dr. Earl Radmacher
President
Western Conservative Baptist
Theological Seminary

Dr. Charles C. Ryrie
Author, Lecturer

Dr. R. C. Sproul
President
Ligonier Valley Study Center

Dr. Charles Stanley
Pastor
First Baptist Church
Atlanta, Georgia

Dr. George Sweeting
President
Moody Bible Institute

*Dr. Howard (Tim) Timmons
Pastor
South Coast Community Church
Newport Beach, California

Mrs. Juleen Turnage
Secretary of Information
General Council of the Assemblies
of God

Dr. Paul Van Gorder
Teacher, Lecturer
Radio Bible Class

Dr. Jack Wyrtzen
Founder, Director
Word of Life Fellowship

*Dr. Thomas Zimmerman
General Superintendant
General Council of the Assemblies
of God

*Participants marked with an asterisk were also members of the North American Overview Committee.

New King James Translation Committee

Dr. Arthur L. Farstad
Executive Editor
New King James Version

Dr. James D. Price
Chairman
Old Testament Translation
Committee
New King James Version

Dr. William H. McDowell
English Editor
New King James Version

‡Dr. James Borland
Professor of Theology and Bible
Liberty Baptist Seminary

Dr. D. David Garland
Professor of Old Testament
Southwestern Baptist Theological
Seminary

Dr. Paul R. Gilchrist
Professor of Biblical Studies
Covenant College

Dr. R. K. Harrison
Emeritus Professor of Old Testament
Wycliffe College
University of Toronto

‡Prof. Zane C. Hodges
Professor of New Testament Literature
and Exegesis
Dallas Theological Seminary

Dr. G. Herbert Livingston
Chairman, Division of Biblical
Studies
Asbury Theological Seminary

Dr. Alfred Martin
Professor of Bible
Dallas Bible College

†Dr. Harry Sturz
Professor of Greek
Biola College

Dr. Curtis Vaughan
Professor of New Testament
Southwestern Baptist Theological
Seminary

‡Dr. Borland and Prof. Hodges joined the New King James Translation Committee after the first printing of the NKJV had been available for two years. The other scholars listed here participated from the 1970's on. The Convocation was chaired by the Executive Editor.

BIBLIOGRAPHY

Books

Arndt, W. F., F. W. Gingrich, and F. W. Danker. *A Greek-English Lexicon of the New Testament.* Second Edition. Chicago: University of Chicago Press, 1979.

Beegle, Dewey. *God's Word into English.* New York: Harper, 1960.

Beekman, John, and John Callow. *Translating the Word of God.* Grand Rapids: Zondervan Publishing House, 1975.

The Bible. A New Translation by James Moffatt. New York: Harper & Brothers Publishers, 1935.

Borland, James A. *A General Introduction to the New Testament.* Lynchburg: University Book House, 1986.

Brown, Francis, S. R. Driver, and C. A. Briggs. *A Hebrew and English Lexicon of the Old Testament.* London: Oxford University Press, 1968.

Bruce, F. F. *The English Bible: A History of Translations.* London: Lutterworth Press, 1961.

_____. *Light in the West.* London: The Paternoster Press, 1952.

Burgon, John W. *The Causes of the Corruption of the Traditional Text of the Holy Gospels.* Arranged, completed, and edited by Edward Miller. London: George Ball and Sons, 1896.

_____. *The Last Twelve Verses of Mark.* Ann Arbor, Michigan: The Sovereign Grace Book Club, 1959.

_____. *The Revision Revised.* London: John Murray, 1883.

_____. *The Traditional Text of the Holy Gospels Vindicated and Established.* Arranged, completed, and edited by Edward Miller. London: George Ball and Sons, 1896.

_____. *The Woman Taken in Adultery.* Reprint. No city: N.P., n.d.

Carson, D. A. *The King James Version Debate.* Grand Rapids: Baker Book House, 1979.

Claiborne, Robert. *Our Marvelous Native Tongue.* New York: Times Books, 1983.

Clark, Gordon H. *Logical Criticisms of Textual Criticism.* Jefferson, Maryland: The Trinity Foundation, 1986.

The Complete Concordance to the Bible: New King James Version. Nashville: Thomas Nelson Publishers, 1983.

Dana, H. E. and Julius R. Mantey. *A Manual Grammar of the Greek New Testament.* New York: The Macmillan Company, 1927.

Demaus, R. *William Tyndale: A Biography.* Revised by Richard Lovett. London: The Religious Tract Society, 1886.

Estrada, David, and William White, Jr. *The First New Testament.* Nashville: Thomas Nelson Publishers, 1978.

Forbush, W. B., ed. *Fox's Book of Martyrs.* Philadelphia: John C. Winston Co., 1926.

Fuller, D. O., ed. *Which Bible?* Third Edition. Grand Rapids: Grand Rapids International Publications, 1972.

_____. *True or False?* Grand Rapids: Grand Rapids International Publications, 1973.

_____. *Counterfeit or Genuine?* Grand Rapids: Grand Rapids International Publications, 1975.

Gesenius, William. *A Hebrew and English Lexicon of the Old Testament.* Trans. by Edward Robinson. Third Edition. Boston: Crocker and Brewster, 1849.

Good News Bible. The Bible in Today's English Version. New York: American Bible Society, 1976.

The Greek New Testament. Edited by Kurt Aland *et al.* Third Edition. Münster: United Bible Societies, 1975.

The Greek New Testament According to the Majority Text. Edited by Zane C. Hodges and Arthur L. Farstad. Second Edition. Nashville: Thomas Nelson, Inc., 1985.

Greenslade, S. L., ed. *The Cambridge History of the Bible: The West from the Reformation to the Present Day.* London: Cambridge University Press, 1963.

Harris, R. Laird. *Theological Wordbook of the Old Testament.* 2 vols. Chicago: Moody Press, 1980.

Harrison, Roland K. *Introduction to the Old Testament.* Grand Rapids: Wm. B. Eerdmans Publishing Company, 1969.

Hills, E. F. *The King James Version Defended.* Des Moines: The Christian Research Press, 1973.

The Holy Bible. A Translation from the Latin Vulgate in the Light of the Hebrew and Greek Originals by Ronald Knox. London: Burns & Oates, 1957.

The Holy Bible. Douay-Confraternity Edition. Los Angeles: C. F. Horan, 1950.

The Holy Bible. A Facsimile of the Authorized Version published in the year 1611 with an Introduction by A. W. Pollard. London: Oxford University Press, 1911.

The Holy Bible. New International Version. Grand Rapids: Zondervan Bible Publishers, 1978.

The Holy Bible. New King James Version. Nashville: Thomas Nelson Publishers, 1982.

The Holy Bible. Revised Standard Version. Second Edition. Nashville: Thomas Nelson, Inc., 1952.

The Holy Scriptures According to the Masoretic Text. Philadelphia: The Jewish Publication Society of America, 1955.

Hort, F. J. A. *Life and Letters of Fenton John Anthony Hort.* 2 vols. London: MacMillan and Co., 1881.

The Jerusalem Bible. Garden City, NY: Doubleday & Company, Inc., 1970.

Koehler, Ludwig, and Walter Baumgartner. *Lexicon in Veteris Testamenti Libros.* Leiden: E. J. Brill, 1958.

LaSor, William Sanford. *Dead Sea Scrolls and the Christian Faith.* Chicago: Moody Press, 1962.

Letis, Theodore, ed. *The Majority Text: Essays and Reviews in the Continuing Debate.* Fort Wayne, IN: The Institute for Reformation Biblical Studies, 1987.

The Living Bible, Paraphrased. Wheaton, IL: Tyndale House Publishers, 1971.

MacGregor, Geddes. *The Bible in the Making.* London: John Murray, 1959.

_____. *A Literary History of the Bible.* Nashville: Abingdon Press, 1968.

McCrum, Robert, William Cran, and Robert MacNeil. *The Story of English.* New York: Elisabeth Sifton Books, 1986.

Metzger, Bruce M. *The Text of the New Testament.* Second Edition. New York: Oxford University Press, 1968.

_____. *A Textual Commentary on the Greek New Testament.* No city: United Bible Societies, 1971.

The New American Bible. Nashville: Thomas Nelson Publishers, 1971.

New American Standard Bible. Nashville: Thomas Nelson Publishers, 1977.

The New English Bible. New York: Oxford University Press, 1971.

The New Testament in Modern English. J. B. Phillips Translation. London: Geoffrey Bros., 1960.

The New Testament: The Greek Text Underlying the English Authorized Version of 1611. London: The Trinitarian Bible Society, [n.d].

Nida, E. A. *Toward a Science of Translation.* Leiden: E. J. Brill, 1964.

Novum Testamentum Graece. 26th Edition (Nestle-Aland). Stuttgart: Deutsche Bibelstiftung, 1979.

Phillips, J. B. *Ring of Truth.* New York: The Macmillan Company, 1967.

Pickering, Wilbur N. *The Identity of the New Testament Text.* Second Edition. Nashville: Thomas Nelson Publishers, 1977, 1980.

Price, James D. *Complete Equivalence in Bible Translation.* Nashville: Thomas Nelson Publishers, 1987.

Rahlfs, Alfred. *Septuaginta.* Sixth Edition. Stuttgart: Privilegierte Württembergische Bibelanstalt, [n.d.].

Rosenthal, Franz. *A Grammar of Biblical Aramaic.* Wiesbaden: Otto Harrassowitz, 1961.

Schaff, Philip. *Companion to the Greek Testament and English Version.* New York: Harper & Brothers, Franklin Square, 1889.

Scrivener, F. H., ed. *The Cambridge Paragraph Bible of the Authorized English Version.* Revised. London: Cambridge University Press, 1873.

Sturz, Harry A. *The Byzantine Text-Type and New Testament Textual Criticism.* Nashville: Thomas Nelson Publishers, 1984.

Smith, J. B. *Greek-English Concordance to the New Testament.* Scottdale, PA: Mennonite Publishing House, 1955.

Tyndale, William, trans. *The First New Testament. Facsimile.* Bristol: N.P., 1862.

van Bruggen, Jakob. *The Ancient Text of the New Testament.* Winnipeg: Premier, 1976.

_____. *The Future of the Bible.* Nashville: Thomas Nelson, Inc., 1978.

Weigle, Luther A. *The English New Testament.* From Tyndale to the Revised Standard Version. London: Thomas Nelson and Sons Ltd., 1949.

_____. "English Versions Since 1611." In *The Cambridge History of the Bible.* London: Cambridge University Press, 1963.

Würthwein, Ernst. *The Text of the Old Testament.* Trans. by Errol F. Rhodes, Grand Rapids: William B. Eerdmans, 1979.

Periodical Articles

Borland, James A. "Re-examining New Testament Textual-Critical Principles and Practices Used to Negate Inerrancy." *Journal of the Evangelical Theological Society,* Vol. 125, December, 1982. Pp. 499-506.

Hodges, Zane C. "The Greek Text of the King James Version." *Bibliotheca Sacra.* Vol. 125, October-December 1968, Pp. 334-45.

_____. "Rationalism and Contemporary New Testament Criticism." In *Bibliotheca Sacra.* Vol. 128, January-March 1971, Pp. 27-35.

_____. "The Woman Taken in Adultery (John 7:53—8:11): The Text." *Bibliotheca Sacra.* Vol. 136, October—December, 1979. Pp. 318-32.

_____. "The Woman Taken in Adultery (John 7:53—8:11): Exposition." *Bibliotheca Sacra.* Vol. 137, January—March, 1980. Pp. 41-53.

Unpublished Materials

Farstad, Arthur L. "The Literary Genre of the Song of Songs." Unpublished Master's Thesis, Dallas Theological Seminary, 1967.

Fisher, Milton C. "The Pattern of Sound Words: An Essential Quality in Bible Translation." Unpublished Review of the New King James version, 1984.

McDowell, William. "Bible Translation and Style." Unpublished monograph, 1983.

Price, James D. "Textual Emendations in the Authorized Version." A paper presented to the Southern Region of the Evangelical Theological Society, March 22, 1986.

Scripture Index